ARMAGEDDON COACH

TEXAS WILL BE THE SITE OF THE LAST PURE HIGH SCHOOL FOOTBALL PROGRAM THE WORLD WILL EVER KNOW

JONATHAN CROMWELL

Copyright

Disclaimer

The information contained in Armageddon Coach is based on the author's personal experiences, research, and opinions. It is intended for educational and inspirational purposes only and is not a substitute for professional advice, guidance, or counselling. Throughout this book, the author has quoted and referenced the work of other writers, coaches, and leaders. Every effort has been made to credit these sources accurately. All quotations are used under the principles of fair use for the purposes of commentary, education, and inspiration. The author and publisher make no claim of ownership over these quoted works.

Many personal stories are shared to illustrate key lessons. In some cases, names, details, or identifying characteristics have been changed to respect privacy. Unless otherwise stated, any resemblance to real persons, living or deceased, is purely coincidental. The author's intent is to honor the people and moments that shaped his journey while preserving the dignity and privacy of those involved.

CONTENTS

ACKNOWLEDGEMENT... i

INTRODUCTION.. iii

CHAPTER 1 7

SICKER THAN AVERAGE 7

CHAPTER 2 17

DO NOT DISTURB.. 17

CHAPTER 3 29

SHIELDING GUARDIANS....................................... 29

CHAPTER 4 47

DISGUISED IN SHEEP'S CLOTHING....................... 47

CHAPTER 5 54

THE ABSENCE OF WISDOM 54

CHAPTER 6 60

THE EROSION OF GRIT IN HIGH SCHOOL FOOTBALL 60

CHAPTER 7 68

DEVELOPING COACHES, ANALYTICS, AND

CONSERVATION... 68

CHAPTER 8 84

FOUNDATIONS, SALARIES, PATIENCE, RETENTION, AND

MOTIVE 84

CHAPTER 9 98

THE BATTLE AGAINST FATHERLESSNESS......................... 98

CHAPTER 10 109

COACHING GENERATION Z LEARNERS 109

CHAPTER 11 131

THE LOST BOYS OF DADDY BALL 131

CHAPTER 12 156

GOD IS REAL.. 156

CHAPTER 13 165

HIDDEN IN THE MEMORIES 165

AFTERWORD... 171

THE 10 TRUTHS OF BEING AN ARMAGEDDON COACH.. 171

ACKNOWLEDGEMENT

To the coaches whose names appear in these pages, and to the countless others whose names do not, thank you. Each of you has left fingerprints on my journey, shaping me not only as a coach but also as a man, husband, and father. Some taught me through victories, others through struggles, and many through the quiet, unseen acts of sacrifice that make this profession extraordinary.

There are far more names and stories than could ever fit in one book, but please know that whether you are mentioned here or not, your impact is deeply felt. Every late-night film session, every word of encouragement to a kid who needed it, every lesson whispered on a practice field—those moments matter. They ripple far beyond a season or a scoreboard.

This book is, in many ways, a tribute to the coaches and teachers who love deeply, lead fiercely, and give more of themselves than anyone will ever realize. You are guardians of the game and of the young lives entrusted to you. I am humbled to be among you and grateful for the brotherhood we share.

To my boys Rocky, Rhett, and Raiden, there is something I want you to know. As we step into the years where I get to coach you, I hope you see how much I love this calling and how much I love the other kids who lace up and play beside you. I hope this book helps you understand what coaching means to me and why it holds such a big place in my heart. But more than anything, I want you to feel how deeply I love you, how proud I am of you, and how important it is to me that you experience pure joy from high school sports.

Rocky, Rhett, and Raiden, nothing makes me prouder than to coach you and also to see other men coach you hard while loving you unconditionally. That is the way coaching is meant to be. When I tell you I love you unconditionally, it means I always will, no matter what happens on or off the field. My love for you has nothing to do with sports or performance. I simply want you to be happy, to know God, and to experience His love even more deeply than I did at your age. To my Sarah, I love you more than you know and I'm so grateful for everything that you do for our family that allows me to coach.

INTRODUCTION

In the heart of Texas, under star-studded skies, lies a tradition that defines the soul of entire communities: high school football. More than sport, it represents a way of life, a sacred passage that testifies to youth's enduring spirit and their mentors' relentless passion.

Texas however, may be witnessing the last bastion of pure high school football. As cultural shifts reshape American priorities, this sacred ground could become the final home of a tradition that embodies the game's true spirit, passion, and camaraderie. Under Friday night lights, we celebrate not just football, but a cherished experience that demands recognition before it becomes merely a beautiful memory.

The essence of Texas high school football finds its perfect expression in Theodore Roosevelt's "Man in the Arena" speech. Roosevelt spoke of the valor, the courage, and the heart it takes to truly be in the arena, to strive valiantly, to dare greatly.

In Texas, the football field serves as that arena, and the coaches and players become its warriors. They are the knights of the gridiron, the unsung heroes who shape destinies, instill values, inspire dreams, and ultimately change lives.

Roosevelt's words echo through locker rooms and practice fields across Texas: "It is not the critic who counts; not the man who points out how the strong man stumbles, or where the doer of deeds could have done them better. The credit belongs to the man who is actually in the arena, whose face is marred by dust, sweat, and blood."

Those who have lived this experience understand what it means to be literally marked by dust, sweat, and blood. They know the profound moment of playing their final Friday night game when a cherished four-year journey transforms into a memory even before leaving the field. In that instant, players realize that what they loved, perhaps occasionally took for granted, has concluded. However, there is a sense of gratitude for having been part of something that others may never fully comprehend

If this resonates with you, then we are the men in the arena, alongside our coaches and their mentors before them, completely distinguished by dust, sweat, and the occasional tear. We lead not for accolades, but because of a love of the game and an unwavering belief in our teammates. As coaches, we guide players toward achievements they might never reach on their own, helping them become men in a world where that path has become increasingly complex.

Every practice, game, and huddle showcases coaches who willingly enter the arena, giving their all so players can learn, grow, and succeed. They drive players home after practice, support them through difficulties, sacrifice time with their own families, and endure criticism from outside forces. Through it all, they remain resilient.

THE TRANSPARENCY OF PURPOSE

To industry leaders, young coaches, seasoned veterans, beloved players, and supportive parents, understand this: there are no secrets to coaching. As Pittsburgh Steelers coach Mike Tomlin says, "The secret is there's no secret." The more transparent we become about our passion and commitment, the better everyone will understand the critical importance of protecting this noble profession.

You may not fully grasp a coach's role in young people's lives today, and that's understandable. My aim is to provide a perspective on this unique profession so you can support it. If you are reading this, you are likely open to exploring ideas that might be overlooked in today's world. I invite you to consider these experiences and share them with others who might gain a deeper appreciation for coaching's vital role.

Coaching transcends employment. It is a calling, but recognizing it as such does not negate coaches' fundamental human needs. Coaching offers the privilege of guiding young people through formative experiences. We are mentors, role models, and oftentimes, surrogate parents. We impart lessons that transcend the field: teamwork, perseverance, resilience, and integrity. This privilege is not guaranteed tomorrow. It is a fragile gift requiring unwavering commitment to preserve.

What we have the privilege of doing is not guaranteed to be here tomorrow. It is a fragile gift that requires our unwavering commitment to preserve, and it hurts my heart to think of a day when we cannot be who we are to so many young people, to each other, and most importantly, to our own families. Coaches' families need their support now more than ever, and I'm here to affirm that it is possible, as it always has been. Though it may take a different form, we need the world to support coaches in every way possible. Allow us to pursue what we love, and we will do it the right way, I promise.

May God open your heart and empower your mind to BE that man in the arena for the people who need it the most. As the saying goes, all good things must come to an end, and high school football, at least as we know it, may prove to be.

For those of us that coach, Texas is the arena, football is the means, and young people are our passion. We stand as ultimate figures in this arena, duty-bound to safeguard this sacred profession and its cherished traditions.

In order to do this, we must remain united, vigilant, and passionate. We owe the next generation assurance that high school football's spirit continues thriving. Help us guard this hallowed ground as torchbearers of a legacy inspiring future generations to step into the arena, dare greatly, and leave indelible marks upon the world.

In the end, it is not the critic who counts, nor the enthusiasm of the sidelines. It is the impact we have on the lives of our players, the bonds we forge, and the dreams we help realize that truly matter. This is the essence of Texas high school football and of high school football everywhere. It is our legacy and culture to define as coaches, and ours to preserve through the trials of time and change. This is our arena, a place where, as Roosevelt warned, "cold and timid souls" should tread carefully.

Coaches have shaped who I am today, transforming my life in powerful, unexpected ways. I remain eternally grateful to all exceptional coaches who have been a part of my journey.

CHAPTER 1

SICKER THAN AVERAGE

The room was thick with disbelief and sorrow, a gathering of diverse souls united by a shared, gut-wrenching loss. It was not supposed to end this way: a tragedy etched into our memories forever. Each of us grappled with the haunting question of what we could have done differently to change the outcome. Naively, I had believed many of these fellow players were invincible, and now, sobbing alongside my teammates was a humbling experience that cut to the core. Just when I believed sorrow could not intensify, it felt as though my soul detached from my body to take one last look at the overwhelming grief surrounding us. It was truly an unforgettable out-of-body experience. My eyes, under the pressure of gut-wrenching pain, could only manage occasional glances, much like watching a catastrophic train wreck unfold. My older brother, Ronnie, was hurt in ways I never thought possible. Ironically, three years later, my time as a player would end in a very similar manner, but with him embracing me instead of the other way around, as it was this time.

The invincible grown men surrounding us were hurting in ways I could never have imagined, their tears fueled by dreams of what could have been. Years of sacrifice, time away from families, and countless hours devoted to our success. All seemed meaningless in that crushing moment. As Texas high school football players, we thought we had given everything to our coaches. Yet that day, we discovered an even deeper reservoir of strength: love. We realized our love for them was greater than we had ever imagined.

A hard-fought game ended with a 19-yard field goal by Stephenville, leaving us stunned and defeated. In front of an electric crowd at Texas Stadium, we had battled the Yellowjacket dynasty as underdogs with everything to prove to Texas, to our city, to all the doubters, and most of all, to ourselves.

I must acknowledge that Stephenville rightfully earned its fourth consecutive state championship that year, a difficult truth that took years to accept. But we truly had them on the ropes and fought fiercely until the final whistle. Both sidelines showcased exceptional coaches, and the field overflowed with warrior-like players who battled relentlessly. Everyone in that stadium understood what was at stake.

Watching the scratchy VHS replay of our team, the Ennis Lions running out of the tunnel at Texas Stadium that day is like watching a scene from an old war movie. Our makeshift entrance, that old gray tarp, the black flaps hanging in front, the trembling PVC pipes that barely held it all together, set the stage for something magical.

The fog enveloped the underclassmen and dads who lined the tunnel outside, anxiously awaiting the reveal. When that black flag with the maroon skull and crossbones finally ripped through the Velcro, it served as our declaration of war. This memory plays in my mind in slow motion: our team striding out like superheroes, fully prepared for battle. The term "superheroes" perfectly captures how we felt each time we emerged from that tunnel.

When I analyze the players' emotions through their interactions with the crowd, their teammates, and their pure, unbridled joy, nothing compares to that stadium entrance. Every single player brimmed with excitement, regardless of playing time. There were no individuals in that moment. Only Lions. The entrance seemed to last forever because we did not want it to end. There was so much joy before the impending clash, and not a single regret among us. Losing this game was never a thought that had crossed any of our minds.

Football is often likened to war, and we can only hope that for players, it remains the closest they ever come to experiencing a real battlefield. The crucial difference lies in what separates sport from true conflict: real war is devoid of happiness, while the exhilaration we felt charging onto that field against Stephenville was undeniably profound.

That excessive happiness was an explosion of built-up emotion, visible to the thousands of fans in attendance. It was electric, a pure moment before the inevitable war on the field. We were, as Notorious would say, "sicker than average," fueled by the passion and fervor within our hearts. We were there to win.

Looking back on that season and the joy it brought, I am so grateful for my coaches. They nurtured us, planting seeds that would eventually flourish, even those I was unaware of at the time. My high school football experience laid the foundation for who I am today.

I like to think of coaches as doctors, prescribing the perfect remedy for past pains, present struggles, and future hardships. Their influence becomes a lasting prescription against the evils of the world that truly heals. I have firsthand experience of this healing power through their involvement in the lives of the players they coach. It is a healing that goes beyond the physical, reaching deep into the emotional and mental aspects of a player's life. The bond between a coach and their players can become one of life's strongest relationships, built on trust, guidance, and unwavering support.

Although it is difficult, I want to share a deeply personal story from my childhood that profoundly shaped who I am and highlighted the significance of high school football in my life. During those years as a player, I was unaware that I was cultivating skills that would benefit me in countless areas of my life.

There is, however, something I need to say first. Mom, I love you. I know you always did your best, and honestly, I think you did an extraordinary job raising us kids. I have watched you navigate us through situations that would have broken lesser people. You could have given up a thousand times, but you never did. Thank you for your unwavering strength. Thank you for being the mother we needed, even when we did not realize how much we needed you.

At around seven years old, I witnessed a family tragedy that altered the trajectory of my life forever. Now, at forty, I watch my own children, who are nearly the same age I was when it happened, and I am struck by an overwhelming question: How does any child process such devastation? What ripple effects would it create in their psyche? How would it shape their journey into adulthood, their approach to marriage, their instincts as future parents?

These are the kinds of profound questions I grapple with now through the lens of experience and parenthood. Back then, as a seven-year-old boy, I was blissfully unaware of the enormity of what I could not possibly comprehend.

Looking back, I realize I was unfairly hard on my mother during certain periods of my youth. It was not until my wife and I became parents ourselves that I began to understand the crushing weight this tragedy placed on her shoulders. The sleepless nights, the impossible decisions, the burden of holding our family together while grieving her own losses.

The image of flames and black smoke engulfing my grandmother's car, with my baby sister inside, left an indelible mark on me as I stood in my elementary school cafeteria, wondering what all the commotion was about outside. I will never forget the sight of flames roaring from that car on that morning.

My grandmother had come to drop off a forgotten backpack we had left behind that morning, and her car was parked just outside my school. I vividly recall feeling a selfish embarrassment when my grandmother burst through the cafeteria doors, screaming, crying, and calling my name as if I could somehow help with whatever was unfolding. I remember calmly getting up from my spaghetti and quietly walking toward all the commotion as administrators and front desk receptionists tried to guide my grandmother back into the lobby area. I had no idea what was coming next.

In the days and years that followed, I was haunted by questions I couldn't answer. Why did this happen? Wasn't there a pair of scissors available to free her car seat from the seatbelt? What could I have done if I had been in the car? What if the backpack hadn't been left at home?

Minutes after I left the cafeteria, I inexplicably managed to escape the chaos of the fire, slipping out the back door of the school as if led away from the unfolding horror by an unseen guardian. I sensed that something was terribly wrong. I remember being alone behind the school, watching the helicopter fly away, somehow knowing its significance as it disappeared behind the tree line that cast shadows over the empty playground. I was too young to understand what a care flight helicopter meant, but I recall leaning against a wooden utility pole next to the swings, wondering what was happening inside and where it was headed. I still look at care flight helicopters today and can't help but think of that day.

More than anything else, I remember the grief we all carried for so long after the accident.

Later that day, I found myself in an unfamiliar classroom with what I assumed was a school counselor, where I eventually painted a picture of a sailboat. That small piece of art remains with me today, a tangible reminder of that surreal afternoon. The goal, I understood even then, was to keep me occupied and distract my mind from whatever was unfolding with my family. So many details from those days have simply vanished from my memory; I remained numb to the world around me for what felt like an eternity.

I do vaguely remember trying to act "okay" in front of the counselors that day, maintaining this facade until it was time to go home. Surely, I reasoned with the logic of a child, if I appeared fine, then everything else would somehow be fine when I returned home. The counselors likely struggled with what to think or say, as they probably knew little about the situation's true magnitude themselves. I suspect they had received minimal communication about what was happening at the hospital, and I certainly had no understanding of what was transpiring beyond those school walls.

In the days that followed, I learned the devastating truth: the flames and smoke had consumed my grandmother's car while my baby sister remained trapped in her car seat. She had been airlifted in that helicopter in a desperate attempt to save her life, but her tiny body had suffered too much damage from the merciless flames. This became one of the most heartbreaking periods of my life, leaving a wound that would forever mark our family.

Katlyn's death forced me to mature with startling swiftness, and for years afterward, I wrestled with trying to comprehend the senseless reasons behind such tragedy. Our family moved abruptly in the aftermath, attempting to escape the well-intentioned but emotionally overwhelming support that surrounded us. Over time, I somehow convinced myself that I had achieved some semblance of normalcy, that I had successfully moved beyond the persistent questions and the haunting thoughts of what might have been different.

The accident occurred close to Christmas, and I have vivid memories of waking up in our new home to find a Christmas tree surrounded by an almost overwhelming pile of gifts beneath it. I can only assume that local churches had organized donation drives to ensure our fractured family could still experience some measure of holiday joy. But no amount of material generosity could heal the profound ache in our hearts or fill the cavernous void we were all experiencing, whether we acknowledged it or not.

I was only seven years old and in second grade when this tragedy struck, far too young to fully comprehend the complex emotions that would follow in its wake. At that age, I was too innocent to question God's role in such suffering. Had I possessed the emotional maturity, I surely would have, but instead, I subconsciously spent years attempting to erase as much as possible from my fragmented memory. Despite these overwhelming circumstances, my mother demonstrated remarkable strength in the years that followed, though we were all broken in ways that defied imagination, and life was often anything but easy.

We rarely attended church during this period, and at that time, I barely knew God at all. Looking back now with an adult perspective, I can see how this experience undoubtedly created significant delays in my spiritual development, a topic I intend to explore more thoroughly toward the end of this book. I find myself deeply grateful for the remarkable protective capacity of our minds during times of intense stress. It is truly amazing how our minds help us adapt and shield ourselves from emotions we cannot process, acting as a cherished defense mechanism.

The following school year, I was held back to repeat the second grade. Looking back now, I never truly questioned this decision at the time, as if I were still emotionally numb to everything that was unfolding around me. Even today however, I can clearly see the earnest benefits of this unexpected turn in my educational journey. The most difficult setbacks I have experienced throughout my life have positioned me perfectly to excel when the right moment arrives. This challenging experience fundamentally reshaped my entire perspective on adversity, like hitting a complete reset button on my understanding of struggle, with the protective haze that followed acting as a necessary shield during my most vulnerable period.

Much like the emotional shield that protected me during those formative years, coaches consistently guide their players through the most challenging times in their lives, demonstrating through their actions and words that a single devastating day does not define who we ultimately become. Instead, the transformative four years of high school football can create powerful generational ripples, profoundly impacting countless lives and fostering exponential positive change that reverberates for years and even decades to come. The best coaches provide a genuine sanctuary where young athletes can safely process and gradually heal from life's most devastating moments.

As this book concludes, I will return once more to the tragedy my family endured years ago, as there is still much I wish to share about that experience and its lasting impact. This painful chapter is just one part of my larger story. I recognize that countless other players across the state are thriving today despite their own setbacks, thanks to dedicated coaches who have instilled them with unwavering support, perseverance, the crucial assurance that "you are good enough," or whatever else was necessary to help them realize their full potential.

Football truly transcends being merely a game. While the sport is certainly filled with inevitable ups and downs, victories and crushing defeats, its most profound power lies in its remarkable ability to unite people in genuinely unique and meaningful ways. Even in our darkest and most desperate moments, we consistently find unexpected light and inner strength through the unwavering support of coaches and teammates who gradually become our chosen family. These coaches from my past hold an especially sacred place in my heart as a living testament to the unbreakable bonds we forge both on and off the field, and how these deep connections help us successfully overcome life's most challenging obstacles. I owe this profound understanding entirely to the exceptional coaches who have so significantly shaped my life and helped lead me steadily towards God.

Even if I am blessed to live to be 90 years old, I know I will never forget that absolutely tragic day in 1990 with Katlyn, and I will always wish with every fiber of my being that I could somehow alter its devastating course. The intense heartache of losing to Stephenville in that crucial 1999 game was ultimately transformed into something genuinely beautiful and meaningful because my coaches approached that crushing defeat in exactly the right way. My coaches turned that defeat into success by consistently instilling sincere love and authentic leadership in every interaction. They left a lifelong impact that sustained me during periods when I was, as they say, "sicker than average" and struggling to find my way forward. The invaluable lessons they taught me through both words and actions continue to resonate deeply within my soul, consistently guiding me to find genuine light even in the darkest moments and offering a type of emotional healing I had not even realized I desperately needed. Texas high school football brings absolutely unparalleled joy to communities across our great state, and I sincerely hope with all my heart that it remains a constant source of inspiration and life-changing opportunity for countless generations of young people yet to come, exactly as it did for me.

Coaches, the profound influence you hold over your players extends far beyond the boundaries of the football field and the confines of Friday night games. The invaluable lessons you consistently teach, the authentic leadership you display through both your words and actions, and the genuine love you carefully instill in each young athlete can fundamentally shape entire lives in transformative ways you may never fully see or completely understand during your coaching tenure. When reflecting deeply on this tremendous responsibility that has been entrusted to you, I encourage you to thoughtfully consider these important questions as you contemplate how your daily actions, critical decisions, and intentional choices profoundly affect the impressionable young people you have the privilege to mentor and guide toward their brightest futures.

COACH'S REFLECTION

- How do you approach moments of failure or loss to ensure they become opportunities for growth and resilience for your players?

- Are you fostering an environment where players feel supported and valued, both on and off the field?

- What steps are you taking to instill not just skills, but life lessons that will endure beyond their time in football?

- How do you personally demonstrate leadership and the values you hope to pass on to your team?

- Are you encouraging your players to find purpose and positivity even in the hardest moments?

Reflecting on these questions can help you reaffirm your role in shaping not just athletes, but well-rounded, strong individuals prepared to tackle life's challenges.

CHAPTER 2

DO NOT DISTURB

In high schools across Texas, certain individuals stand out not because of their physical stature or administrative authority, but because of their profound ability to shape young lives. These extraordinary figures are coaches who move through the hallways with an unmistakable aura that ignites passion and purpose in their players. They serve as far more than motivators; they function as architects of personal growth, methodically instilling core values, inspiring genuine hope, and consistently demanding excellence from every student they encounter. Their love manifests as fierce and unconditional action rather than mere sentiment, becoming evident in every grueling practice session, every high-stakes game, in every victory, in every loss and every invaluable life lesson they impart. These dedicated professionals nurture not just skilled athletes but complete human beings, generously pouring their hearts into their students, their players, and yes, even sharing their undeniable love for Whataburger.

This chapter serves as both an ode to the cathartic impact of coaches and a timely reminder of their remarkable ability to influence lives far beyond the superficial distractions that dominate today's digital landscape. It also functions as an urgent call to action for coaches everywhere to pause and engage in meaningful reflection, encouraging them to step away from the relentless gravitational pull of social media platforms and refocus their energy on what truly matters: building authentic, lasting relationships with their players. These genuine human connections hold infinitely greater meaning and value than the fleeting likes, shares, and digital validation we too often find ourselves chasing in our online lives.

Eminem once reflected, "If I could remove just one thing from the world today, it would be the internet." He expanded on this thought, explaining, "With the internet, so much about fundamental humanity has changed in ways we're still discovering. If it didn't exist, people helping children on the street would do so because they genuinely want to help, not to record and broadcast it for social media validation. Artists would be recognized and celebrated for the actual quality of their creative work, not because a major label promoted them heavily through sophisticated online marketing campaigns. The internet has facilitated the spread of countless negative influences throughout our society. Today, people can become famous for virtually anything, which isn't always beneficial for our collective well-being. Without the internet, the world would likely be more peaceful, and we could experience life authentically, away from the constant pressure of cameras and public scrutiny. I genuinely miss the late 1990s, when I personally signed CDs and shipped them directly to fans, creating real, tangible connections."

While the idea of a world without the internet may sound romantically idyllic, it remains far from realistic in today's rapidly evolving, technology-driven society. Digital technology has become permanently woven into the fabric of our daily existence, continuously reshaping how we communicate with one another, acquire knowledge, and navigate our personal and professional lives often at the cost of personal connections and isolation. A promising and encouraging shift, however, is beginning to emerge within educational systems: the implementation and enforcement of comprehensive policies that restrict student phone usage during school hours. These thoughtful measures have the potential to create essential space for deeper, more meaningful connections and truly undistracted learning opportunities that young people desperately need, even when they fail to recognize this need themselves.

Because everything they know in this world has been regulated by technology and media, our current generation of youth can not fully grasp or understand the profound and lasting impact that constant technological immersion has had and is having on their psychological and social development. From the earliest moments of their lives, digital devices have systematically fostered a pervasive sense of isolation that masquerades as genuine connectivity. Dr. Jeremy Nobel, a respected lecturer at Harvard Medical School, articulates this phenomenon succinctly: "Just as thirst serves as a clear biological signal that you need hydration, loneliness functions as an equally important signal that you need authentic human connection." As leaders, educators, and mentors in young people's lives, we must fully acknowledge and address this troubling reality. Our young people did not consciously choose to grow up during this hyper-connected yet paradoxically isolating era. Instead, they were dealt a challenging hand that has left them more personally disconnected than perhaps any generation in recorded history, despite living in what appears to be the most technologically connected time humanity has ever experienced.

This isolation has real consequences. Research shows that loneliness can be as harmful to health as smoking 15 cigarettes a day. Let that sink in: the mental and emotional toll of loneliness rivals the physical damage caused by smoking. Decades ago, tobacco companies marketed cigarettes as harmless—going so far as to recruit doctors and dentists to endorse their products. Slogans like "Just What the Doctor Ordered" misled the public, and during World War II, free cigarettes were even included in soldiers' rations to keep them hooked. When research in the 1950s began linking smoking to cancer, tobacco companies doubled down on their marketing to protect their profits.

It is genuinely chilling to consider that we may currently be witnessing a remarkably similar phenomenon unfolding with digital technology and social media platforms. Over the past twenty years, children and adolescents have been exposed to completely unprecedented levels of technology usage, and I predict that the long-term mental health impacts will eventually become undeniably clear and impossible to ignore. One day in the not-so-distant future, we may look back with regret and realize we did not fully understand the extensive psychological harm being inflicted on developing minds, just as older generations now reflect with remorse on a time when children could casually purchase cigarettes for nineteen cents at the local neighborhood pharmacy.

What is happening to our youth is real, and the solution is not in more technology but in fostering genuine human connection. This is where coaches play an extraordinary role. Their influence goes far beyond the scoreboard. Coaches shape character, resilience, and a sense of belonging in ways no algorithm ever could. Join me in recognizing and celebrating these dedicated mentors, because they hold the power to create lasting, meaningful change in the lives of the next generation.

It is time to shift the focus back to what truly matters: relationships that transform lives.

Coaches are, in essence, real-life influencers. However, unlike the social media influencers who dominate today's digital landscape, coaches wield a fundamentally different kind of influence, one that is far more powerful and enduring. Their impact cannot be measured by followers or likes, but rather by the profound and lasting transformation they create in individual lives. In a world where the term "influencer" has become synonymous with someone who commands thousands of online followers, coaches represent something entirely different: they are exceptionally potent micro-influencers operating in the truest and most meaningful sense of the word.

Although coaches may not boast tens of thousands of followers across platforms like Facebook, Instagram, or X, they possess something infinitely more valuable: the genuine respect, trust, and admiration of those they guide and mentor. Their influence stems not from viral content or carefully curated posts, but from authentic relationships built through consistent support, guidance, and investment in others' growth. These coaches cultivate a truly authentic following and generate generational ripple effects that compound throughout entire communities, creating waves of positive change that extend far beyond any single interaction or moment in time.

A quick internet search reveals that a micro-influencer maintains between 10,000 and 50,000 followers. In stark contrast, even the most dedicated coaches, who might mentor 75 new players each season throughout a 40-year career, will directly influence at most 3,000 individuals. This number falls significantly short of the 10,000 followers required for official recognition as a micro-influencer.

In the digital realm, most influencers, while there are certainly notable exceptions, tend to create largely superficial impressions on their audiences. They often drive impulsive purchasing decisions, promote body-enhancing products of questionable value, or encourage unrealistic lifestyle transformations that rarely lead to lasting change.

A coach's priority, however, has never been about accumulating numbers; rather, it centers on the depth and enduring quality of their impact. Coaches, by contrast, impart something far more valuable and enduring: wisdom earned through experience, courage cultivated through adversity, and genuine love that transcends transactional relationships. These are qualities that no algorithm can replicate, no filter can enhance, and no engagement metric can truly measure. The influence of a great coach extends far beyond follower counts, creating ripple effects that shape character, build resilience, and inspire generations of athletes to become not just better players, but better human beings.

Social media has revolutionized communication, creating platforms where audiences gather but often fail to connect. Technology has altered how we express love and appreciation, replacing genuine interactions with virtual gestures that look the same regardless of the person. However, the deepest forms of love and influence occur face to face, through shared experiences and personal growth that come from in-person interaction. Coaches have the unique opportunity to foster genuine relationships daily, demonstrating to their players the essence of true care and commitment. When digital ones supplant face-to-face interaction, something crucial is lost. The absence of an authentic connection creates a void that even the most captivating digital presence cannot fill. This shift can lead people to construct and believe a false narrative that not only must they appear perfect to others, but also that everyone else is more perfect than they could ever realistically be.

I consider myself a marketing guy. I have always been fascinated by the way small businesses grow, but what I want to focus on here is something deeper, something heavily researched, refined, and perfected daily by mega companies: **aspirational marketing.**

Our world constantly pushes this narrative, conditioning many of us to view ourselves in a diminished light. Aspirational marketing relentlessly delivers the same message: you are not enough. Sometimes it is a direct nudge to buy now. Other times, it is a subtle seed planted, preparing you for what they will sell you next.

This is the reality young people face every single day. A reality reinforced by influencers, by the media, and by nearly everything they consume.

On the other side of this narrative stands the coaching profession. Coaches work tirelessly to counteract this conditioning. Instead of telling players they are lacking, we remind them of their inherent worth. We meet them where they are, honor where they come from, and guide them toward where they want to go. Growth, in this sense, is not about becoming someone different. Growth means cultivating happiness, building confidence, and strengthening the values that allow them to one day pass this mindset on to their children.

Over the years, I have often told my players what my true hope for them is: lasting success. But I do not define success the way the world does. To make it clear, I'll say, *"If I see you in Walmart 20 years from now, I want to see someone who is genuinely joyful and fulfilled. I want to see peace in your eyes."* I want them to be at peace and I want to see it in their eyes!

The joy I'm describing isn't tied to wealth, physical appearance, or superficial ideals. It has nothing to do with being rich, handsome, wrinkle-free, slim, or having a full head of hair. True joy begins in the heart, yet if you look closely, you'll always see it reflected in a person's eyes.

Dr. Gabor Maté often references Bronnie Ware's profound book *The Top Five Regrets of the Dying*, which captures the honest and vulnerable reflections of people looking back on their lives. According to Ware, the most common regret was this: *"I wish I'd had the courage to live a life true to myself, not the life others expected of me."* Dr. Maté highlights this truth to show how frequently we abandon our authenticity to meet societal expectations or to win approval, only to find ourselves diminished in the process.

The second most common regret was, *"I wish I'd had the courage to express my feelings."* Dr. Maté draws attention to this point to emphasize how the suppression of emotions can take a deep toll on our health, both emotionally and physically. As he explains, *"The repression of the authentic self and the suppression of emotion are both significant contributors to chronic stress and illness."*

These insights remind us of something essential: a meaningful life is not about chasing someone else's version of success. It is about having the courage to be true to ourselves, to express what we genuinely feel, and to protect our emotional well-being. When we live in alignment with who we are, joy flows more freely, and that joy becomes visible not just in our hearts but in the way our eyes shine with peace and authenticity.

As coaches, our mission extends far beyond developing players on the field. Our true aspiration is to guide them toward lives filled with happiness and fulfillment, regardless of their income, physical appearance, or worldly achievements. We encourage them to center their attention on what genuinely matters in the grand arc of life, and to release the distractions that so easily entangle them, such as the endless pursuit of followers and likes on social media.

When I reflect on my time with some of the greatest coaches I have known, one thing becomes unmistakably clear: they lived by two principles that many people, later in life, wish they had embraced much earlier. First, they valued players for who they were, offering acceptance without condition. Second, they forged deep emotional connections, bonds strengthened by the shared passion for football. In truth, football is only the vessel. The real purpose lies in the lasting impact we have on shaping lives. The game itself may fade with time, but the values, confidence, and sense of belonging we instill in our players endure, often becoming the foundation of their happiness long after the final whistle is blown.

This digital age brings with it a plethora of distractions, including but not limited to: social media, mobile phones, tablets, smart watches, video games, and countless more. As our world becomes increasingly digital, the yearning for authentic human relationships grows stronger. No matter how many likes, shares, or hearts appear on a screen, they can never replace the depth of real human connection.

Unchecked, these digital distractions can spiral into anxiety and depression, pulling players away from their true purpose and leaving them restless in pursuit of meaning. The ultimate assignment in life is to love one another, yet this timeless truth often becomes clouded by the noise of modern life. What many perceive as a desire for "something more" is often not a genuine need at all but a void of the heart and mind that frequently gets filled by addictions of every kind. In my view, this technology-induced emptiness has become the root of addiction for many today, as people chase fulfillment in places where it cannot be found.

Coaches, much like vigilant sheepdogs, are acutely aware of these dangers. We see how swiftly distractions can infiltrate the lives of players, and how easily they can creep into our own lives as well. To guard against this, coaches navigate the digital landscape with care. Many find balance by keeping close circles of trusted friends and companions, while others gravitate toward platforms such as X (formerly known as Twitter), where they connect with like-minded individuals and fellow coaches who share a positive outlook. In these intentional spaces, they find community, perspective, and the strength to keep their mission clear.

THE IRONY OF TECH LEADERS AND SCREEN TIME

An intriguing and often ironic dynamic exists within the tech industry when it comes to screen time and children. Despite being architects of the technology that dominates modern life, many tech industry leaders take starkly conservative approaches to screen use in their own homes.

For instance, Steve Jobs, co-founder of Apple, admitted in a *New York Times* interview that he limited how much his children were allowed to use the iPad at home. Likewise, Bill Gates revealed that he enforced strict screen-time caps and prohibited his kids from owning mobile phones until the age of fourteen, as reported by *Business Insider*.

This cautious stance extends well beyond Jobs and Gates. Many Silicon Valley executives deliberately create tech-free zones in their homes, setting firm boundaries between work and family life. Writing for *Forbes*, Maren Bannon notes how these leaders often stress the dangers of social media in particular. One executive bluntly stated, *"The real evil is not the smartphones but social media,"* pointing to the addictive nature of certain apps rather than the devices themselves.

Taken together, these insights reveal a striking truth: the very architects of our digital world acknowledge the powerful pull of addictive algorithms and the unhealthy habits they can create in children. Ironically, while the rest of society struggles to manage its relationship with technology, many of the industry's top leaders are already working to protect their own families from the very tools they helped bring into existence.

Recent discussions have drawn attention to possible links between screen time and developmental disorders such as ADHD. One tech billionaire even claimed that his child's ADHD symptoms were reversed simply by reducing his child's exposure to screens, as reported by *Times Now News*. While the validity of such claims remains debated, the story underscores a growing awareness of how digital consumption can affect children's mental and cognitive health.

The irony is undeniable. The very people who design and innovate digital experiences are often the same ones who impose the strictest limits on their use at home. They know firsthand how persuasive and at times destructive modern technology can be, which forces them to live in tension between being creators and protectors. This awareness underscores the importance of approaching technology with intention, especially when shaping the lives of children. To call technology harmful almost feels insufficient. It is not merely a distraction; at times, it can be a genuine threat.

This is where coaches can and should step in. Coaches provide players with the tools needed to rise above the noise: joy, purpose, hope, wisdom, courage, and above all, love. These are the gifts that elevate coaches beyond the shallow influence of digital personalities. Coaches create a refuge for their players, a sanctuary where they can step away from the chaos and focus on what truly matters.

In a world consumed by the loudest and brightest distractions, coaches guide players to see beyond the immediate, teaching them the enduring value of hard work, discipline, and dedication. We encourage them to metaphorically hang their *Do Not Disturb* signs, carving out spaces free from external pressures and influences. Within this environment of calm, players can form deeper connections, discover profound insights, and grow into men and women of integrity.

Above all, coaches teach the essence of joy, not as fleeting happiness, but as the calm assurance of God's unwavering victory. Often, this lesson is absorbed without players even realizing it has been taught. That is the heart of real influence.

It is important to recognize that these modern distractions may be diluting the powerful role coaches play in young lives more than we fully realize. In the midst of chaos, strong leadership becomes essential, offering both the calm that diffuses anxiety and the confidence required to move forward.

Great coaches understand that their ultimate purpose is not simply to win games, but to shape men and women of character—individuals who will grow into loving spouses, devoted parents, and, in some cases, inspirational coaches themselves. Texas football, in many ways, serves as a modern-day arena where these battles for values are fought.

In this setting, coaches stand as guardians of principles that often seem increasingly at odds with the world around them. They labor tirelessly to instill these values in their players, just as their own mentors and coaches did for them. These efforts are rarely reflected in analytics, statistics, or scoreboards. Instead, they are etched into the lives transformed and the legacies that endure long after the final whistle.

This book guides you to become an exceptional coach, revealing what it truly takes to connect with players. It aims to uncover the inherent strengths within every coach, shaped by their own mentors.

Ask yourself: Would your mentors be proud of the coach you are today? Would they encourage you to be more courageous, more devoted to your players, and more committed to your family? Whatever your answer may be, remember this: every coach has room to grow and the potential to surpass even their own expectations.

To step into this calling, coaches must look beyond the X's and O's of strategy and rediscover the very passion that made them fall in love with the game in the first place. Coaching requires patience, trust in the process, and an appreciation for the beauty of the journey itself. While players today may appear different on the surface, at their core, they remain the same. They long for guidance, understanding, and someone who genuinely believes in their potential.

As this chapter draws to a close, pause to reflect on the distractions competing for your attention as a coach. Consider how you might clear away these distractions so you can focus on what truly matters. Reach out to fellow coaches. Connect with those from other states, rival coaches, youth coaches, and future coaches. Together, let us uphold and champion the values of love, integrity, and excellence, instilling these principles in future generations of players and, in turn, the coaches they will inspire.

Embrace your role as a true influencer. Not one measured by followers, likes, or fleeting recognition, but by the lasting legacy you create in the lives you touch.

COACH'S REFLECTION

Take a moment to reflect on your role and the principles outlined in this chapter. Consider the following questions to guide your thoughts and evaluate your impact as a coach:

- Are there distractions in your personal or professional life that prevent you from focusing on your core values as a coach? How can you address them?

- How do you actively demonstrate love, integrity, and excellence in your interactions with athletes, peers, and the community?

- What steps are you taking to connect and collaborate with other coaches, both within and outside your circle, to grow and share knowledge?

- How are you ensuring that the lessons you teach extend beyond the field or court and leave a lasting imprint on future generations?

- If someone were to describe your legacy as a coach, what would you hope they say about your influence and character?

Reflect deeply and honestly. Your answers will shape not only your growth but also the countless lives you touch along the way.

CHAPTER 3

SHIELDING GUARDIANS

In a Willie Nelson song, he sings, "My heroes have always been cowboys." My heroes have always been coaches—those steadfast individuals with whistles around their necks and an unshakable sense of purpose. I spent nearly a decade coaching high school football before writing this book, and during that time, I developed a profound understanding of what coaches truly are: guardians. They are protectors who guide their players on and off the field, offering not just strategy but mentorship that shapes character and resilience.

During my years of coaching, I witnessed firsthand the dedication and passion that coaches pour into their work. They do far more than teach plays; they safeguard their players, helping them navigate life's challenges and offering a steady hand when they stumble.

I'm back to coaching now, but even during my eight years away from the sidelines, the title of "coach" always filled me with pride. "Coach" is more than a role. "Coach" is a responsibility to nurture young athletes into strong, principled individuals. In high school football, the real competition is not confined to the field. The deeper contest is about shaping integrity, building character, and instilling the resilience needed to face life's battles. While the final score may settle a game, coaches ensure their players leave the field equipped to tackle the challenges of the real world.

Recently, North Alabama Head Football Coach Brent Dearmon shared a powerful message on social media that drove this truth home. In his post, he pulled back the curtain and revealed a glimpse of the unseen struggles coaches walk through alongside their players each week—struggles that extend far beyond wins and losses.

"What most people never see:

- Grandmother passed away

- Grandfather passed away

- Grandmother had a stroke

- Assistant coach's father hospitalized

- Wife undergoing radiation treatment

- Parents divorced after leaving for college

- Car repossessed

- Father laid off from job

- Mother borrowed player's car because hers broke down

- Brother had a trial back home

- Car accident

- Player discovered with enlarged heart

- Career-ending injury

- 12 injuries

- Stranger broke into a player's house while they were asleep

- Player working night shifts

- Family member kicked out of the house
- Family member released from prison after being wrongly accused

"And we yell at them to 'make the play!'

WE BETTER LOVE, SERVE, AND CARE."

Reading this reminder underscores just how little the X's and O's truly matter compared to the deeper purpose of coaching. Reading this list reminds me of just how much the X's and O's pale in comparison to a coach's real purpose. The role of a coach is not simply about winning games; it is about standing as a protector, offering support, compassion, and guidance to young athletes navigating life's trials. Coaches are the unsung heroes, the guardians of hearts and minds, shaping lives far beyond the football field.

Evil is a choice, often made in the absence of courage. Within these pages, you will come to see that coaches are, in many ways, the enemies of evil. They work tirelessly to diminish its influence on every player they encounter, fully aware that each day brings all of us closer to a moral reckoning.

As Dr. Gabor Maté explains in his book *The Myth of Normal*, much of what society labels as "normal" is neither healthy nor natural. It has only been normalized because the majority accept it or experience it as such. Coaches recognize this truth and push back against the false standards imposed by culture, reminding players that real strength lies in authenticity, integrity, and courage.

Maté writes, "What we call normal is a product of repression, denial, and disconnection," compelling us to thoughtfully question the systems we readily accept and to examine their genuine effects on our collective well-being. The meaningful relationships that coaches cultivate with their players prove absolutely crucial for shaping the future of our society. These dedicated mentors remain acutely aware of the destructive forces that actively seek to undermine these sacred bonds, yet they also understand that Texas high school football possesses both the essential tools and the unwavering resolve necessary to stand firm in this ongoing battle.

Ephesians 6:10-18 serves as a profound and powerful reminder of the spiritual warfare "Finally, be strong in the Lord and in his mighty power. Put on the full armor of God, so that you can take your stand against the devil's schemes. For our struggle is not against flesh and blood, but against the rulers, against the authorities, against the powers of this dark world and against the spiritual forces of evil in the heavenly realms. Therefore, put on the full armor of God, so that when the day of evil comes, you may be able to stand your ground, and after you have done everything, to stand. Stand firm then, with the belt of truth buckled around your waist, with the breastplate of righteousness in place, and with your feet fitted with the readiness that comes from the gospel of peace. In addition to all this, take up the shield of faith, with which you can extinguish all the flaming arrows of the evil one. Take the helmet of salvation and the sword of the Spirit, which is the word of God. And pray in the Spirit on all occasions with all kinds of prayers and requests. With this in mind, be alert and always keep on praying for all the Lord's people."

Throughout my years in sports, I have had the privilege of being coached by numerous remarkable men, where I got to watch these men firsthand stand up against this evil that I'm referring to. These coaches, unwavering in the face of challenges, are the backbone of every successful team but also a staple in their respective communities that fairly enough love them just as much as they love them back. Among them, Coach Paul Willingham from Ennis, Texas, shines brightly as a model of leadership and integrity. For over four decades, Coach Willingham has been a guiding light in our community, his presence on the field synonymous with love, respect, and an indomitable spirit.

More than twenty years have passed since I played my last high school football game, and while Coach Willingham may have gained a few gray hairs, his passion for the game and his players remains unchanged. Known for his raspy, passionate country accent, his booming voice echoes across the field, filled with love and urgency. His old black Ennis football hat, a cherished relic, symbolizes his enduring commitment to the years of memories that he has spent coaching football and loving players. Every practice was a new adventure, with Coach Willingham keeping us on our toes, whether through unexpected drills or some good old-fashioned motivational "hollering". His unpredictable nature kept us sharp, ensuring we approached each day with renewed vigor. Beneath this tough exterior however lays a deep reservoir of love and dedication that he poured into every player.

In my second year of coaching, I worked with the defensive line at Ennis High School, alongside many coaches I deeply admire and respect. It was a truly eye-opening experience. Fueled by passion and a genuine desire to make an impact, I approached the role with enthusiasm, even as I continued to find my footing as a young coach. It was also my first year at Ennis, a place that holds a special place in my heart, where I had once played football and built so many cherished memories. Returning as a coach, I was determined to honor that legacy and inspire the very journey I had lived as a player. Among my players that year was a talented yet deeply troubled senior, a young man who needed more guidance than actual coaching. Despite my efforts to build a relationship with him, tensions often rose, fueled by his struggle to handle accountability. I will never forget one particular game when frustration reached its peak. As we headed into the locker room at halftime, he snapped at me. In that moment, I found myself completely unprepared for how the player bursted out, my own emotions were dangerously close to boiling over.

In hindsight, I realize that my lack of understanding of his behavior played a significant role in how the situation unfolded. Had I followed through with what I was about to do in that heated moment, I could have escalated things far beyond anything I intended. It was one of those pivotal crossroads where, without restraint, everything could have spiraled out of control, possibly leading to irreversible consequences for my career as well as the players' development. Now, with greater awareness of the world we live in and a deeper understanding of how the enemy of our souls operates, I see just how close I came to making a costly mistake. Thankfully, by God's grace, it did not turn out that way.

Thankfully, Coach Willingham was nearby, and what unfolded next was nothing short of a masterclass in leadership. He did not plead with the player; instead, he asserted respect where it was due, confronting him with a presence that was both fierce and loving. With calm authority, he stepped in and defused the tension, balancing wisdom with empathy. His voice carried the intensity of a lion, yet it was tempered with compassion, delivering a message that was raw, genuine, and impossible to ignore. And when it was finished, it was finished. No lingering arguments, no need for explanation. The moment carried its own weight.

Willingham had earned this influence long before I joined the staff as a coach. His relationship with the player had been forged over years of trust, consistency, and mutual respect. That foundation gave him the ability to reach into the heart of the situation and connect in a way I simply could not. He knew things about this young man I could never have known, and he understood the patterns behind his behavior in ways only time and experience could reveal. His wisdom and steady presence shielded both the player and me, highlighting the profound difference a true leader can make. His insight and guidance were invaluable, showcasing the power of leadership rooted in deep knowledge and trust. Witnessing his intervention felt like watching a father protect his son, providing the support I had not realized I needed at that moment. He was a guardian, shielding and imparting wisdom into my heart in ways I could only appreciate as a coach, not as a player.

Reflecting on this experience, I am reminded of Dr. Gabor Maté's insights on trauma and the way it shapes human behavior. He explains that our reactions often rise out of unresolved wounds, not simply from what is happening in the present moment. My inability at the time to truly comprehend that player's actions may have been connected to struggles and experiences deeply rooted in his past. Recognizing this later helped me see that behavior is rarely as straightforward as it first appears. There was far more taking place in that young man's heart than anyone could see on the surface. As a young coach, I sensed some of this but lacked the wisdom and maturity to properly navigate the emotions that defined that night.

Today, I understand that in our world, with pressures coming from all directions for both coaches and players, this situation could have easily turned into a career-ending experience. It is the kind of scenario where the devil triumphs, and my face might be broadcasted on the local news as the "villain," a coach who got physical with a player. While I acknowledge that some teachers and coaches occasionally cross boundaries, I often find myself wondering what went wrong when I see far too many unfortunate stories about coaches and players making headlines. I ponder whether stronger leadership could have averted the situation. It does not take much. Simply stay vigilant to the devil's traps and steer clear of them at all costs!

Another exemplary figure who shaped my life is my high school offensive line coach, Wayne Walker. During our thrilling playoff runs as the Ennis Lions, he consistently encouraged us with his distinctive country twang, declaring with unfaltering confidence, "Somebody's going to win a state championship… it might as well be us!" This powerful mantra, delivered while wearing his characteristic big floppy fishing hat, represented far more than mere words. It embodied his relentless drive and genuine passion for both the game itself and every single one of his players.

Coach Walker demonstrated a tireless dedication that knew no boundaries, frequently sacrificing precious family time and life's simple pleasures in service to his team. He remained completely unwavering in his commitment to his players, staying fully aware of the profound and lasting impact he was making on our young lives. Together, we forged unforgettable memories and pursued collective greatness as a unified team. He consistently showed us authentic love in every possible setting, whether on the demanding practice field or during chance encounters at the local grocery store. Walker's genuine love has remarkably endured through more than forty years of devoted coaching, touching countless lives along the way.

During my freshman year, I experienced a heartbreaking tragedy that left an indelible mark on me. Coach Walker and our team lost one of our own. A young man, a good soul, who fell victim to the devastating grip of drugs. His life came to a tragic end at a city park in our town after getting entangled with the wrong crowd. At the time, my brother and I were new to Ennis, uncertain of our future in football and still learning what it meant to be part of a team destined for greatness. Witnessing this tragedy and Coach Walker's response to it became one of my earliest and most profound lessons in the extraordinary dedication of the Ennis coaching staff. At the time, I could acknowledge it, but it took me years to fully understand the depth and significance of how he managed it with us as players.

Coach Walker's heartbreak was palpable. He carried the weight of that loss with him, and even twenty-five years later, it remained a subject that stirred deep emotion within him. I remember vividly how often his eyes would well up whenever the memory of that young man resurfaced. Looking back now, I realize that Coach Walker was carrying as much of the pain as he could in front of us, not only for himself but also for us as his players. He allowed us to see his vulnerability, repeatedly and unflinchingly. As a young person, I found it deeply healing to see such raw humanity in a man I deeply admired.

He was present in his grief, unafraid to lay it bare before us. His pain was authentic, and in those moments, the distance between coach and player disappeared. We were no longer separated by titles or roles. We were simply a grieving family, bound together by the weight of loss and the comfort of shared sorrow.

Words fall short of capturing how much Coach Walker means to me or how much joy he has brought into the lives of so many others. He truly embodies the light described in 2 Corinthians 4:6-18: "For God, who commanded the light to shine out of darkness, hath shined in our hearts." Coach Walker is a living example of that light, shining even in the darkest moments, and for that, I will always be grateful.

Coach Walker's influence goes far beyond football. He and his wife, Sandra, became guardians in our lives, welcoming us into their family with open arms. Sandra made their home a haven for us, nourishing us, supporting us, and always understanding the demands of her husband's role.

Their children, too, welcomed us with open hearts, even when it must have been difficult to share their father with a team of young athletes. There is something about the Walker family that has always felt like a shelter, a place of peace that steadies the soul. It was never just Coach Walker who cared for us; his entire family embraced us as if we were truly their own.

I did nothing to earn that love. I was simply blessed to cross paths with them and to be folded into the warmth of their lives. To the Walker family, I can only hope that this book serves as a reflection of the deep gratitude we hold for your parents. Their quiet, selfless love guided and shaped us in ways that words will always struggle to fully express.

To me, these coaches were more than mentors, they were shielding guardians. They will always hold that place in my heart. They are Armageddon Coaches.

THE UNSUNG HEROES OF GUARDIANSHIP: COACHES' WIVES

In sports, the spotlight often shines on players and head coaches, the ones most visible in moments of victory or defeat. Yet behind every great coach stands an unsung hero: their spouse. These remarkable individuals embody love, sacrifice, and unrelenting support, not only for their partners but also for entire teams and communities. They form the quiet foundation that holds everything together in the demanding world of coaching.

As players, we often took for granted the relentless drive of Coach Walker. Through grueling practices, blistering heat, and the mental grind of two-a-days, he constantly reminded us to keep our eyes on the bigger picture: the ultimate prize. His floppy fishing hat became iconic, shielding him from the sun as he radiated both energy and joy. What we did not realize at the time was that Coach Walker was pushing himself just as hard as he was pushing us. Coaching is not only physically exhausting; it is emotionally draining as well. In retrospect, there were certainly days when he longed to be at home with his family, yet he never allowed us to see that side of him. He made it all appear effortless, and for that, we owe him a lasting debt of gratitude.

Yet behind Coach Walker's strength and leadership stood Sandra Walker, the heart of it all. She was not only his wife but also a second mother to many of us. Sandra welcomed us into her home, fed us, and treated us like family. Her unwavering support allowed Coach Walker to pour his full energy into the team, while her kindness and generosity shaped us both as players and as young men. Together, the Walkers operated as a seamless unit, offering us a living example of what true partnership looks like. Their love and dedication were a gift that reached far beyond the football field.

Being part of a coach's family is never easy. The long hours, the emotional weight of wins and losses, and the countless sacrifices are realities few can fully understand unless they have lived it themselves. Coaches' spouses like Sandra carry these burdens with grace, often setting aside their own needs to uplift their families and communities. Sandra shared her husband with us, and their children shared their father with us, offering more of themselves than we could ever repay. Those years remain among the best of my life, and I will always be grateful for the Walkers kindness, their selflessness, and the lessons they passed down to us on and off the field.

I hope the Walker children, along with the children of every coach, have the chance to read this. I want them to know that the countless hours their parents poured into us were never in vain. For me, their efforts did far more than shape my life. They continue to ripple forward, touching the lives of my children and, in time, will influence future generations as well.

This story isn't unique. Many coaches' wives carry the same weight, balancing the demands of their husbands' careers while embracing the players and team as if they were their own. After Georgia's National Championship win, Coach Kirby Smart credited his wife for sharing in the victory, acknowledging the emotional burden she had carried throughout the season. Their triumph was not his alone; it belonged to both of them.

A coach's life is all-consuming, demanding sacrifices that extend far beyond the sidelines. They miss family dinners, school events, and countless moments at home. Their wives step in to hold everything together, becoming the foundation that keeps the family strong. Misty Houston, a coach's wife and former president of the Texas High School Coaches Wives Association, once described "loaning" her husband to the team. She offered care to every player because, to her, they mattered just as much as they did to him. That selflessness reflects the quiet strength and compassion required to be part of a coaching family.

Coaches' wives are far more than silent supporters. They are guardians of their households and, in many ways, guardians of the team as well. Like protectors standing at the gate, they shield their families from the strains of the profession while creating a sense of belonging for players. They learn every player's name, every backstory, and every struggle. From the stands, they cheer with the same passion they would show their own children. And just as a guardian absorbs the blows meant for others, they take on the emotional highs and lows of the season. When the team celebrates victory, the family celebrates too. When the team endures defeat, they shoulder that pain together.

Sandra Walker's story captures this balance with striking clarity. She embraced her husband's passion for coaching and, in doing so, extended her love to the team, welcoming the players as if they were her own. Her example reminds us that coaching is never just a job; it is a shared calling. It is a communal effort where love, sacrifice, and commitment create the environment in which young athletes are able to thrive. Like steadfast guardians, the wives of coaches remain vigilant, ensuring that the values of care, resilience, and perseverance ripple through both their families and the teams they support.

The role of coaches' wives has changed significantly over the years, especially in today's world. Many no longer come from generational coaching families, and as a result, they may face a steep learning curve when adjusting to the unique demands of the profession. This shift can create difficulties for younger coaching families as they navigate the demanding nature of the profession. By building strong support networks and offering resources, we can help these women adapt and thrive, ensuring their families and teams succeed in this all-encompassing path.

Coaches' wives fill a role that extends far beyond the sidelines. They help shape team culture, influence the lives of young athletes, and leave behind legacies rooted in love, sacrifice, and support. While their contributions often go unseen by the public, they remain indispensable to the sports world. It is crucial to recognize the evolving dynamics of coaching families and provide support for the next generation of coaches' wives, enabling them to continue being pillars of strength for the athletes, their husbands', and their own families while operating harmoniously with the life of a football coach.

At the same time, we must acknowledge the equally pressing responsibility of the profession itself. Now more than ever, it is essential for head coaches and leaders in the coaching community to embrace innovation and remain vigilant in the search for better productivity tools. Coaching is not just about hard work; it is about working smarter. We must be willing to adopt new strategies that improve how we approach our roles, especially during the demanding stretches of work that consume weekends and evenings. Winning will always matter, but efficiency and balance matter just as much.

By streamlining processes and eliminating outdated practices that linger only because "that's how we've always done it," coaches can reclaim valuable time. That time should not only be spent refining player performance but also invested at home, where coaches hold the equally important role of being mentors, leaders, and examples for their own families.

I learned valuable lessons about effective teaching in sports from my own coaches. Drawing from my experiences as a player, a young coach, and my subsequent studies, I've dedicated myself to understanding player development and refining the initial phase of the coaching workweek: reviewing the last game and evaluating players. Through repeated trial, error, and adjustment, I have been able to drastically streamline this process and others. But I've come to realize something important: I've only scratched the surface.

The more I learn, the more I recognize opportunities to create better workflows and eliminate wasted time caused by disconnected systems. None of the progress I have made relies on X's and O's; instead, it comes from addressing inefficiencies and strengthening the connectivity between platforms.

Here is the reality: our families deserve better. By taking a closer look at how we operate, we can align our processes with the needs of modern coaches, making the profession more sustainable for the next generation. This is not only about improving work-life balance; it is about ensuring that coaching families, including spouses, children, and loved ones, receive the time, care, and attention they truly deserve.

To me, these women remain the unsung heroes behind every victory, both on and off the field. My wife, Sarah, is the heart of our family. Her strength, love, and support inspire me every single day. Together, we have built a home grounded in respect, compassion, and accountability, values we are intentional about passing down to our children. Sarah's influence is immeasurable; she is the steady hand, the guiding voice, and the glue that holds us together.

Like so many coaches' wives, her legacy is not written in public recognition but in the quiet power of love and partnership. It is a reminder that greatness is rarely achieved alone, because it is built on the foundation of those who stand faithfully beside us. I love you, Sarah, and I hold deep affection for the entire Willingham and Walker families, more than words could ever express!

To every family within the coaching profession, know that you hold a rare and invaluable opportunity to guide and mentor the players entrusted to your care. Embrace this responsibility wholeheartedly, and do for them what someone once did for you.

ODE TO THE CLASSROOM GUARDIANS

There's a part of this book I wrestled with more than once. I cut it out, put it back in, and edited it repeatedly. The reason is simple: I want to honor Andrea Webb without leaving any confusion about why her story belongs here. She was my tenth-grade English teacher at Ennis High School, and her example still echoes in my heart more than twenty years later. Her guardianship in the classroom reflects the same spirit I have been describing throughout this chapter, the spirit of a true coach.

This section is also for every teacher who does not wear a whistle or stand on a sideline but still carries the same calling. Band directors, math teachers, English teachers, science teachers, and countless others know their subject is secondary to the relationships they build and the lives they touch. Like great coaches, they understand that what matters most is the heart of the student in front of them.

For me, Mrs. Webb embodied that truth. I was not a bad kid, but I was tired, overworked, and unprepared far too often. Between football, schoolwork, and a forty-hour work week, I often showed up to her class running on empty. Sometimes I fell asleep at my desk. Sometimes I was not ready for a test. She always knew. She saw through me. She knew what I had not read, what I had not studied, and where I was falling short.

What still amazes me is that she never lashed out in frustration. She did not embarrass me or treat me like a student who did not care. She held me accountable, and I earned every seventy I scraped by in her class. But she gave me something deeper: grace. She understood that English was not my real battle in that season of life. She knew my heart, and she gave me what I needed most, unconditional love and patience during a time of exhaustion.

And then came the day that revealed her guardianship in a way no one could ever forget. Two years after the Columbine shooting in Colorado, that same indescribable terror some would call evil walked into her classroom. A former student entered carrying a loaded gun and demanded that the students line up against the inside wall. Instead, the students instinctively gathered at the front of the room where Mrs. Webb sat at her desk.

With the gun pointed directly at her, she stood up. The young man ordered her to leave, but instead of fleeing, she walked in front of her students, positioning herself between them and the gun. When ordered again to leave, she said no. She refused to abandon one student for the sake of another. She stood her ground with a fierce love for everyone in that room, including the gunman. She even tried to convince him to hand over the weapon before any harm was done.

He refused her offer, despite her willingness to exchange herself as a hostage for the others. In the end, he allowed all the students to leave the room except for one, whose life Webb ultimately protected. Her courage was the light in a room quickly filling with shadows, and her love saved lives that day.

The next morning, Webb came back to school. She parked in her usual spot, walked through the front doors, and returned to the same classroom where everything had changed. She paused outside for a moment, opened the door, turned on the lights, and finished the school year with her students. For eleven more years, she taught in that same room. That classroom was her arena, and she never stopped fighting the good fight until the day she retired.

The tragedy of that day still lingers. Trauma always does. Yet so does her legacy. What she modeled was not just courage, it was unconditional love in its purest form. Though a young man's life ended in senseless tragedy, countless others were forever shaped by the way she chose to respond.

Andrea Webb will never ask for recognition. She does not want trophies or headlines. But for me, and for so many others, she is a legend. She is proof that the calling of a teacher can be every bit as powerful as the calling of a coach. In fact, the calling is the same. What many do not understand is that the instincts, character, and heart of teachers who do not coach are identical to the best coaches. They see through weak leadership. They understand accountability. They are gritty to the core. They know how to meet kids where they are. They despise favoritism, and most importantly, they fear God.

Andrea Webb is, without question, an Armageddon Teacher.

Looking back now, I see clearly what she gave me. While my community celebrated championships, Mrs. Webb knew I was closing a gas station after midnight on Fridays, working weekends, and trying to keep up with football and school. She knew I was stretched thin, but she also knew my heart. She gave me grace when I needed it most.

This tribute is not just for her. It is for all the teachers who fight the same fight in their own classrooms. You are the guardians. You are the salt of the earth. Coaches love you because we know you speak the same language we do: the language of love, accountability, and unwavering presence.

Andrea Webb will always be a guardian to me. She showed me what it looks like when unconditional love meets unshakable courage. And in a world that needs more light, her story reminds us why we need teachers and coaches who see beyond the scoreboard or the gradebook and into the hearts of the kids they serve.

Mrs. Webb recieved the Carnegie Medal of Heroism for her actions on May 15, 2001

COACH'S REFLECTION

Reflect on the lessons your heroes passed down to you and how their influence shapes your coaching. Perhaps it wasn't a coach, but a parent, friend's parent, older sibling, teacher, manager, neighbor, or spouse. By honoring their legacy through your actions and values, you create a ripple effect that nurtures growth, resilience, and leadership in the next generation. Who were your heroes?

- Who are the people who have supported, guided, or inspired you through life's challenges?

- How can you show gratitude to those who have positively impacted your journey, either directly or through small gestures of appreciation?

- How can you carry forward the values of strength, love, and dedication modeled by your heroes into your coaching practices?

- What steps are you taking to embody the principles of mentorship, resilience, and leadership that your heroes demonstrated?

- If someone were to describe your legacy as a coach, how would you hope they view the impact you've made, both on and off the field?

CHAPTER 4
DISGUISED IN SHEEP'S CLOTHING

You are about to read my best attempt at describing something nearly indescribable on its grandest stage: the evil inside education that is deeper and more invested in deceit than we are willing to admit. While names will not be mentioned, many of you will automatically think of certain faces as you continue reading. Some of you may even grit your teeth or find that you are clinching your fists rather than dwell on old hurts, misunderstandings, and damage you might feel these people have inflicted, however, I urge you as teachers and coaches to stay strong in your faith and recognize that our true adversaries are not the flesh and blood individuals who may come to mind, and would like to encourage you to pray for and forgive those people so that we can focus on what is truly important. The day may come when they may need us, and we must be prepared to be there for them.

In this chapter, I want to shed light on one of the greatest challenges facing high school sports and the growth of careers in the coaching profession. Let me be clear about something. The purpose of this book reaches far beyond what many of the so-called "cold and timid souls" could ever comprehend. My goal is to bring light to a few along the way, or at the very least, to earn a nod of agreement from those who recognize the truth in my perspective. That which we can call nothing other than "Evil" manifests in various forms, sometimes as catastrophic as famine, sometimes as personal and destructive as murder, theft, hatred, or abuse. At other times, evil reduces us to silence at times when we should call out something that we know is wrong, when we should rise in protest of injustice and inhumanity , when we should raise our voice in support and encouragement of those we see struggling. Every inch of our world is in the crosshairs of where evil wants to exist, including public and private education. Often, this thing called evil is disguised in sheep's clothing, masking negative intentions that support an agenda the individuals might not even recognize influencing them.

This "evil" in education, as I define it, is any harmful force that seeks to undermine, sabotage, or destroy what is beneficial for children. Charles Baudelaire, a great 19th-century French poet, famously said, "The greatest trick the Devil ever pulled was convincing the world he didn't exist." However, I once heard a different perspective: that the Devil's greatest trick was convincing the world that good did not exist. This alternative view emphasizes a world rampant with hopelessness.

My understanding of this "evil" is that if it recognized the immense power and influence of the coaching profession and the generational impact coaches have on young people, it would launch an all-out attack. Its goal would be to minimize, invalidate, or dishonor the impact coaches and teachers have on their players.

I'll argue that this "evil" does fully comprehend the good coaches bring to our world, and its attack is happening before our very eyes. "Evil" seeks to extinguish the good and advance its agenda and self interests, while coaches tirelessly plant seeds of hope and love. They're natural enemies, like donkeys and coyotes. Look that up!

In today's society, coaches are usually held to a higher standard of behavior and personal conduct both on and off the playing field because they are often viewed as heroes and role models for the young people with whom they work. They have the power to shape not only their athletic abilities but also their character and values. Coaches serve as mentors, teachers, and leaders to their players, instilling in them important life lessons that go far beyond the playing field.

The impact of an effective coach can be seen in every aspect of a player's life - from their work ethic to their attitude towards challenges. Coaches push their players to become better versions of themselves both physically and mentally. They teach them about teamwork, sportsmanship, resilience, and determination - all crucial skills .

In the last chapter, I shared a story from my second year of coaching that centered on a player who lost his temper just as we were heading in for halftime. At first, I wondered if that story carried enough weight to illustrate the struggle against evil. But in truth, it was the perfect example. Many of you might have thought about how you would have "put that player in his place." Honestly, had I been the reader rather than the writer, I would have thought the same thing. I am that guy, competitive, passionate, and committed to coaching kids to reach their full potential.

What I want you to understand, though, is that the story was never about losing my cool. It was about recognizing how evil often tempts us in the most ordinary moments. These small lapses, losing your patience, giving in to anger, letting pride dictate your response, become the cracks through which far greater damage can slip in. Such moments are everywhere, hidden in plain sight, waiting for the right time to catch us unprepared. And that is exactly how evil operates: cunningly, deceptively, and relentlessly in its pursuit.

In today's world, there's little care for context when things don't go as planned while "getting after a kid." The timid souls can't do this the right way because they don't understand relationships as we do. With established relationships, we can hold players accountable on and off the field. We've been through this ourselves as players and we know the importance of balance. In the heat of the moment, it is crucial to remember the importance of fostering strong relationships with players, ensuring they always feel valued and supported. As coaches, we must be able to push our players to reach their potential, but just as importantly, we need to manage the aftermath with care and understanding. Balancing discipline with empathy is key to building trust and growth.

This often involves subtle yet impactful actions, and frequently requires an exponential approach. This could mean catching a player for a one-on-one talk, making direct eye contact with a nod of approval, or waiting for the player to initiate the next exchange. When your players know you love them, it gives you the freedom to coach them with intensity and purpose.

Building relationships takes time. In that heated moment with my player, I had nothing to gain by escalating the situation since the relationship wasn't there yet. Evil would have been the only winner, potentially manifesting in various forms I'm thankful never materialized. It could have led to unnecessary negative emotions, physical altercations, or words that couldn't be taken back. Situations can escalate quicker than we realize, and I'm grateful this one didn't. True leadership can intuitively recognize such situations and defuse them effectively, preserving relationships and, at times, even careers.

Building strong relationships with players and parents is more important now than ever before. We are men coaching young men, all passionate about what we do. Frustration and heated moments are part of the game. Like any family, it isn't always perfect. Life does not unfold with perfectly balanced emotions or neatly scripted responses. As coaches, we know that if there is no healthy level of friction, then we are not doing our job. Evil often sees that friction as an opportunity, sending the message that coaches should never be tough on players. But we know better. Discipline and accountability are not only essential for growth, but also for shaping habits and values that will serve our players long after their playing days are over. In the real world, there is little room for idealistic notions about how this generation "should" be treated. An inability to handle accountability will eventually cost someone their job and, in turn, place their family in a difficult position. Failing to grasp the value of accountability and consequences robs players of that spark in their eyes, draining the joy I spoke of earlier in Chapter Two.

As a coach, I have witnessed both strong and weak leadership in education. Weak leadership is not necessarily evil, but it often feels aligned with evil at its highest levels. For school districts, identifying strong leadership is crucial, yet many outside of education struggle to understand what that truly looks like. Choosing not to stand against negative influences is, in effect, choosing to become part of the problem. True educational leadership supports teachers and coaches, making the right decisions even when it is tough, instead of bowing to public opinion or advancing personal gain. True leadership is about developing others, maintaining meaningful relationships, and embracing opposing views. It is about standing firm and not being swayed by status or job security. It is about genuine love and organization, standing the test of time, and focusing on quality over quantity. True leadership is resilient and nurturing, and it must be what we strive for in Texas high school football.

Not standing up to evil - anything or anybody that undermines or sabotages something good for students - means becoming a part of it. Evil is not supporting a teacher when an unfair parent wants them stoned in front of the school. Evil is not supporting a coach when he starts one player over another because it is the right move, even if it can't be supported with meaningless statistics. Evil lets the community dictate your next move, hoping your contract will be renewed. Evil allows another person's career to be destroyed over a situation you could have de-escalated if you had a backbone. Evil applauds our choice to remain silent when seeing something - or someone - unjust, cruel, hateful, demoralizing, or dehumanizing. Evil gives us permission to avoid contact and communication with those we know are dealing with trauma, loss, loneliness, pain, and struggles. Evil pads resumes with weak degrees, checking boxes only to climb toward the next position. Evil walks into staff development in August expecting a red-carpet welcome. Evil chooses status over developing others into stronger leaders for the future. Evil acts as if it has arrived and forgets where it came from.

Evil - that which undermines, sabotages or damages goodness - cannot form genuine, lasting relationships; instead, it clings to connections it believes will lead to the next promotion. Evil leads with bias, shutting out opposing views. It sees those views as a threat and an inconvenience rather than an opportunity for growth. Evil feels entitled to job security it has not earned. Evil is trained to interview well and give answers without substance, a polished façade hiding emptiness. Evil knows how to charm school board members and newspaper reporters while keeping close watch on the good-hearted people who threaten its false image.

Evil cannot not give unconditional love for evil is self-serving, ego-driven, and incapable of honesty, trust, support, and forgiveness. That which is touched by Evil becomes tainted and weakened, and unable to stand the test of time because it values numbers over quality, quantity over impact, the superficial over substance, the prize over the person. Because of this, Evil is hollow, knowing neither victory nor defeat. Such Evil cannot be welcome in any Texas high school football program or game and should not be ignored at any level within the education system. Countering the powerful influence on and potential damage to the young people with whom we work requires, I think, constant self-examination and commitment to being constantly aware of all that is happening around us, our players, our game. The source of the undermining, the sabotage, the damage, if you will, comes like the wolf disguised in sheep's clothing, but when the mask slips, when the glitter tarnishes, new reality is one of viciousness, pain, and cruelty, one of injustice, prejudice, hatred, and intolerance. It is an understatement to say I cannot stand the word. Like most of you, I have been lulled into complacency by those wearing the mask and I have been burned when the glitter turned to ashes. For the most part, I have recovered from the wounds, but the scars remain, ever a reminder of what happens when goodness is undermined and sabotaged by those who put self interests above all else.

As coaches and men of the arena, we can never forget that the evil we face often hides in plain sight, masquerading as something harmless, something profitable, something that strokes our egos. It is determined to distract and seduce us, ultimately aiming to destroy what we know to be honorable and true. Only through resilience, strong relationships, and unwavering principles, can we overcome them. Our focus must remain on nurturing our players and leading with integrity, ensuring these destructive influences have no place on our teams or in our lives.

COACH'S REFLECTION:

Have you ever faced a moment in your coaching career that felt emotionally charged? Think back to an encounter with a player or parent that could have taken a wrong turn.

- What did you learn from that experience?
- How did you navigate the emotions involved, and what strategies helped you maintain a positive outcome?
- In what ways can you extend support to other coaches and their families who may encounter similar challenges?
- What insights from your journey can you share to inspire and guide others in their coaching practice?

Reflect on these questions to deepen your understanding and enhance your impact as a coach.

CHAPTER 5
THE ABSENCE OF WISDOM

In today's rapidly evolving world, obtaining a doctorate without the wisdom to apply it effectively has become alarmingly common. Unfortunately, the emphasis on degrees, accolades, and resumes has turned them into critical checkboxes that districts and board members prioritize when considering candidates. These "paper airplane trophies" have overshadowed the much-needed investigative and creative interview processes essential for genuinely assessing potential leaders. While continuous learning is crucial for becoming better leaders, a doctorate does not automatically equate to being a better superintendent than that candidate who did not have one. Countless exceptional leaders have been overlooked simply because they did not possess an impressive array of formal credentials during the interview process. In this chapter, I highlight the profound value of wisdom over credentials and explore how this shift is shaping the fields of coaching and education as a whole.

The focus needs to return to evaluating candidates based on their leadership skills, character credibility, and moral integrity—qualities that are often overlooked because they are harder to quantify. Yet, these "intangibles" are precisely what matter most, especially to coaches who understand their critical role in driving success. Execution, effort, and accountability on the field often stem from these intangible traits, even though they do not show up on stat sheets. For the coaches reading this, I'll mention that my software, WARDBORD, is specifically designed to measure these essential intangibles!

When it comes to hiring leaders for school districts or electing school board members, we should prioritize these same attributes, giving them the freedom to make decisions rooted in these vital qualities. Unfortunately, the current process often relies heavily on paper qualifications and a narrow set of conventional attributes, which candidates are expected to present before even being considered. This overreliance has fueled the widespread use of external hiring firms that prioritize credentials over authentic leadership potential, all while draining valuable district resources. It is time to rethink how we define and assess leadership.

Hiring the best candidate for critical positions like superintendent, athletic director, and head coaches are undoubtedly a daunting responsibility fraught with challenges. It requires the courage to ask tough questions and the resolve to support decisions collectively, even when they conflict with popular opinion. Decision-makers must stand firmly by their choices, even if it means not selecting the candidate with the loudest voice in the community. To ensure a more complete evaluation, decision-makers must look beyond résumés and degrees. They should consider a candidate's leadership journey, the mentors who have influenced them, and the values that shape their approach. For leadership roles, I strongly believe that interview panels should ask the following key questions:

1. "Can you share three examples of individuals whose growth and development you have supported? How long have you known them, what paths did you help them pursue, and what are they achieving now? May we speak with them?"

2. "Who do you credit the most for your personal growth? And professionally, who has had the greatest impact on your development?"

True leaders will answer these questions with ease and enthusiasm, as these are topics they are deeply passionate about. Their responses will offer valuable insight into their ability to inspire growth in others and their own journey of development.

Winston Churchill once said, "I am your servant. You have the right to dismiss me when you please. What you have no right to do is ask me to bear responsibility without the power of action." This sentiment resonates today as authority is increasingly stripped from leadership roles. Public service entails responsibilities that come with expectations and accountability, yet, it must also include the authority to act and enforce accountability. Without that authority, outcomes will always fall short, no matter how many motivational posters are hung on the walls or how many inspirational speakers are brought in. Teachers, coaches, and law enforcement officials know this struggle well. Too often, their hands are tied by top-down decisions that undermine their ability to act effectively. Stripped of authority, even the most dedicated leaders cannot fulfill the responsibilities demanded of them.

Evil has a game plan, and it often reveals itself through the removal of authority, leaving those in the arena of leadership unable to act. These flaming arrows strip away the empowerment educators and coaches need to make meaningful decisions. Those of us who teach and coach all know this feeling. We have all experienced it, and many of us can likely relate to it right now. Too often, decisions to remove authority are made as a substitute for standing up for what is right.

The difficulty of standing firm in today's world, especially at the level where many decision-makers operate, is that doing so almost always invites conflict. And conflict, for them, often feels like an unwelcome distraction from the comfort of a secure office and a padded bank account, but making difficult decisions in favor of what is right is essential for true progress. Seeking wisdom from experienced mentors can provide the perspective needed to navigate these challenges with discipline and grace. Leaders must recognize that their choices directly shape the future, demanding not only courage but also faithfulness to their calling.

As coaches, we cannot and will not surrender the authority tied to the discipline and responsibility entrusted to us. We must expect accountability from those who share our values in developing young people, and we understand that we are the ones called to carry out this mission every day. Undermining the authority of coaches and teachers is more than a troubling trend. It is a destructive force that must come to an end.

Evil is reshaping the way we teach, pushing methods onto teachers and coaches that are neither a good fit nor truly beneficial for students and players. One of the most important decisions an administrator can make as a leader is to acknowledge that while new research may seem intriguing, it is often wiser to hold off on implementing it until it is proven and ready. I borrowed this concept from Coach Chip Kelly, who emphasized the importance of knowing when to hold back on running a new play if the team is not ready.

Coaches understand this mindset well. Every day, they make decisions based not on what looks impressive on a dry-erase board but on what gives their players the highest probability of success. I can admit without hesitation that I have seen tons of coaches who could outdraw me on a whiteboard. But the difference is this: they couldn't get their kids to play as hard as mine, and when the game is on the line, that difference shows. They lose. I win. Every time. The truth is, being able to explain your strategy in a meeting room means little once the whistle blows. What matters most is the ability to inspire players to give everything they have. And when that moment comes, my players will outwork and outlast yours.

The well-being of students and the success of teachers should be the primary concern of leadership in education. New initiatives should enhance teachers' capabilities, not hinder them. Legendary educators and coaches have proven their ability to learn and grow; therefore, any new initiative must be carefully considered to ensure it genuinely supports them. By valuing genuine leadership over credentials, maintaining authority for effective action, and making thoughtful decisions that prioritize the needs of teachers and students, we can create an environment where both educators and learners thrive. I am frustrated by the prevalence of unqualified individuals in leadership roles, placed there not by merit but because they had the right connections or credentials.

Imagine if educational leaders approached decision-making with the same caution and care as a seasoned coach deciding whether to introduce a new play. The trust, faith, and leadership required would need to be exceptional, ensuring that decisions enhance rather than hinder educational success. This approach could help redirect the current trajectory toward a more purposeful and beneficial path for both educators and students.

At its core, education exists to foster growth and development. By making sound decisions and supporting our educators, we can ensure this purpose is fulfilled for both current and future generations. Leadership must be recognized not as a title but as the responsibility to make wise, impactful choices that serve the greater good. In doing so, we can overcome the flaming arrows of evil and create a future where both educators and students thrive. Seek wisdom when faced with difficult decisions; there is always someone more experienced who is willing to help.

Detroit Lions head coach Dan Quinn once shared his perspective on "nice" coaches, stating that being nice is not what defines a great leader. Quinn emphasized that true coaching is about setting high standards, holding people accountable, and pushing them to realize their full potential, even if it involves hard conversations or tough love. His approach highlights that effective leadership stems from authenticity and a commitment to growth rather than a desire to simply be liked. This wisdom demonstrates how leaders, like coaches, wield influence through their actions and decisions, often offering lessons that are not immediately understood or appreciated. It is a reminder that leadership, much like coaching, requires both resilience and resolve to bring out the best in those you guide. That brings me to the topic of toughness and what it truly means from a coach's perspective when it comes to players today.

COACH'S REFLECTION:

As you reflect on this chapter, consider the following questions to deepen your understanding and practice:

- How should leaders today move beyond traditional credentials to identify and nurture true leadership potential within our teams?

- What strategies can we use to empower leaders to make bold, meaningful decisions that align with our core values?

- How can we create an environment where open dialogue and principled stands are welcomed, even when they challenge the status quo?

- Are we consistently prioritizing the needs of both teachers and students in our decision-making processes? If not, what changes can we make?

- How can we design new initiatives that remain flexible and adaptable to the unique needs of our educational community?

Take time to reflect on these questions and consider how they align with your current practices and goals as a coach.

CHAPTER 6

THE EROSION OF GRIT IN HIGH SCHOOL FOOTBALL

In recent years, society has witnessed a concerning shift: the rise of entitlement and a growing softness. This cultural change, marked by a lack of resilience and an inability to cope with adversity, has seeped into many areas of life, including high school football. A sport once defined by grit, determination, and fierce competition now faces challenges from these societal shifts that threaten its core values. Football, like life itself, is meant to be demanding. Life is not easy; it is more like a dance, full of rhythm, missteps, and moments of growth.

I vividly remember my freshman year at Ennis, when I played defensive line and practiced with the JV team. For a young player at a football powerhouse like Ennis, that was a big deal. My older brother Ronnie, a junior at the time, was a relentless and dominant offensive lineman. He played the game the right way, with intensity and precision. When he was the pulling guard on a counter play, he would demolish the defensive end, clearing the path for the tackle, wrapping around to take out the linebacker. Ronnie led the way for our running backs, and he always brought the hammer. Watching him set the tone on the field left a lasting impression on me.

The following year, Coach Willingham, our defensive coordinator, traded me to Coach Walker to play offensive line. At first, I hesitated. As a young and inexperienced player, I mistakenly believed I could "hit more people" as a defensive lineman. But that hesitation did not last long. Ronnie had already laid the groundwork, showing me what it truly meant to play offensive line with both skill and physicality. He set the standard high, and I aspired to meet it.

Looking back, my freshman year was a pivotal time. Practicing and competing alongside older, more experienced players on a highly competitive and physical team pushed me to my limits. By the end of the season, I was near my breaking point. I would not say I was soft coming into freshman football, but I certainly wasn't the same person when it ended. I was shaped by the grind. As a freshman, I was not fighting for a varsity starting spot, but I was practicing with them. On a championship-caliber team like ours, those practices were anything but easy. There was no room for sunshine, rainbows, and unicorns.

I'll never forget one practice late in the season. I was completely spent, emotionally and mentally. My body ached from the long season, my spirit was worn from the pressure of keeping up with older, stronger teammates, and I was drained from trying to appear tougher than I actually was. I was sore all over, with no one to blame but myself, as Chris Stapleton might sing.

That is exactly how it should be for young people. They are meant to be challenged in ways they never imagined, pushed to their limits and beyond. Along the way, they will experience pain, both physical and emotional. But it is in that struggle, in that discomfort, where real growth happens. Football taught me that lesson, and I'll always be grateful for it, even when it came with sore muscles, bruised egos, and bloody calluses. Those experiences shape us and bind us as teammates.

At the time, we do not always realize what we are going through. Each of us faces the same grind in our own way, sharing something extraordinary, something most people will never fully know or understand. That shared struggle builds unspoken bonds.

I still remember one particular day when I felt completely drained, beaten down in every sense of the word. I thought I was hiding it, masking my emotions behind the typical "tough guy" act. But I was not fooling anyone. Ronnie, my teammate and big brother, saw right through me. Later that evening, he came up to my bedroom. I do not know how he knew what I was feeling, but he did.

He sat down and, in the way only a big brother can, encouraged me. I'll never forget how he quoted the chorus from John Michael Montgomery's *Life's a Dance*.

"Life's a dance, you learn as you go
Sometimes you lead, sometimes you follow
Don't worry 'bout what you don't know
Life's a dance, you learn as you go."

Ronnie was not wrong. That moment meant more to me than he will ever know, and it would have never happened without football.

Football is tough, but life is tougher. Being a husband, a father, an employee, or a boss does not make things any easier. Yet football prepares you for that grind. It teaches resilience, discipline, and the camaraderie needed to face challenges head-on. It is hard, undeniably so, but I can not imagine facing life without the lessons I learned playing football at Ennis. Those lessons stay with players forever.

H. L. Mencken once said, *"Every normal man must be tempted, at times, to spit on his hands, hoist the black flag, and begin slitting throats."* That quote captures the essence of high school football, a spirit of relentless drive and tenacity. Back in the day, Coach Steve Marrow instilled in us a lasting truth: success demands hard work, sacrifice, and an unwavering will. He taught us that greatness requires being ready to fight, endure pain, and push past limits. The blood, sweat, and tears from those grueling workouts were not just struggles; they were rites of passage that molded champions.

There is immense value in outworking your opponents and investing fully in the culture of teamwork and brotherhood. Coach Marrow is known as the quiet, soft-spoken coach whose words carry weight whenever he speaks. His wisdom and fierce love for his family are evident, and he is a devoted man of God with a special passion for special teams. He often led weekly character lessons for the team, always approaching us with confidence in our abilities and a genuine affection that shone through his ever-present smile. Coach Steve Marrow is the epitome of kindness and a tireless champion of what is good in the world. He embodies grit and determination, but does so with a calm, steady presence, showing his players that true strength does not need to shout to be felt. Through his quiet confidence, he teaches that being heard comes from authenticity and purpose, not noise.

While I acknowledge that times have changed and improvement is necessary on many fronts, I believe grit remains a defining trait that will always set individuals apart, no matter how soft the world becomes. Life will always demand that we fight for jobs, protect our families, defend our marriages, uphold justice, and stand firm in our beliefs; including our faith in God, but today's culture of entitlement is eroding that mentality. Many young athletes expect success to come easily, without the sacrifice and effort required to earn it. They shy away from challenges, diluting the competitive spirit that we all love so much about high school football fields across the country. Comfort and convenience have begun to overshadow the drive to overcome adversity. In prioritizing safety over strength, we lose the opportunity to embrace both.

The truth is, there will never be a time when you should not be capable of standing up for yourself or your loved ones if necessary. Whether you are a player on the field or a parent navigating the road with three car seats in the back, you deserve to have that edge. Embrace the chaos and take on the challenge. It is not about picking fights with everyone around you, but there is value in carrying a bit of danger as part of the adventure. For the record, I've never been in a fistfight and consider myself nonviolent, but let's just say I know how to be dangerous if I need to be.

It is challenging to articulate, but the sense of entitlement I see today is evident even before games begin. Players run out of the tunnel with an air of self-entitlement, influenced by today's world and the rampant idealism of self-promotion over the "team first" mentality. I do not highlight these issues to criticize today's players but to encourage reflection on the current state compared to the high school football I once knew. It is not the fault of young athletes that they were born into this modern world however, it is their responsibility to discern what they need to learn and which beliefs will endure.

Look at the most successful sports programs, and you will find an absence of selfishness, a culture of grit, and friction from coaches who promote strong character. These elements are the most impactful experiences football can offer. High school football is more than just a sport; it is a microcosm of life, teaching lessons that extend far beyond the field. The challenges, the victories, and even the defeats are all integral to building character.

In this new era, coaches, parents, and players must recognize the value of these lessons. While the world may change, the principles of hard work, resilience, and selflessness should remain constant. As the landscape of sports evolves, maintaining a balance between progress and tradition is essential. Embracing innovation while holding onto time-tested values can ensure that high school football continues to be a beacon of character development. I am here to say that everything I learned from my experience at Ennis and being part of two state championship teams remains true to this day. Winning it all still requires the same dedication, discipline, and hard work. There are no shortcuts, and you can not afford to be soft if you want to achieve greatness in life.

Young athletes should be encouraged to embrace the discomfort that comes with growth. Coaches play a pivotal role in creating environments where players can push their limits and discover the true meaning of grit. It is about instilling in them the understanding that adversity is not an obstacle but an opportunity.

The importance of a "team first" mentality cannot be overstated. Self-promotion may be prevalent today, but the power of unity and collective effort is unparalleled. Successful programs thrive on cooperation and mutual support, where each player's success contributes to the team's success.

High school football now stands at a crossroads. The challenge lies in adapting to modern times without losing the principles that shaped the game's foundation. By prioritizing character, resilience, and teamwork, high school football can continue to shape future leaders. Young athletes must learn that success is never handed out. It is earned through dedication, sacrifice, and perseverance. The same grit that defines champions on the field is the grit that will serve them throughout their lives.

Though entitlement and softness may be on the rise, the enduring values of high school football can push back against these trends. The game teaches that the road to greatness will always be demanding, but it is a journey worth taking. Through football, young people discover the power of commitment, the value of teamwork, and the strength of character required to succeed in any arena.

Compounding the issue of entitlement is a growing lack of loyalty within the football community. New coaches often show little allegiance to the districts that hire them, jumping from one opportunity to the next in search of better prospects. Players, too, have become transient, frequently transferring to different schools in pursuit of greater exposure or perceived advantages. This instability disrupts team cohesion and undermines the sense of community that is vital to the sport's success.

This lack of loyalty is intertwined with a sense of player entitlement and a preference for the quick and easy fix over long-term commitment. There is an overall lack of grit when it comes to putting in the work and trusting the process of player development. Instead of investing time and effort into building their skills and perseverance, both players and coaches often seek immediate results. Yet, as Galatians 6:9 says, *"Let us not become weary in doing good, for at the proper time we will reap a harvest."* This verse serves as a reminder that dedication and persistence are essential to true success in football, and indeed, in every other aspect of life.

Leadership within districts also bears responsibility. Administrators sometimes prioritize short-term gains over long-term development, making decisions that destabilize programs and erode trust. This lack of steadfast leadership creates an environment where loyalty is undervalued, further weakening the foundation of high school football.

The vacuum left by this erosion of loyalty and resilience has given rise to external influences that are reshaping the narrative of high school football. Youth football leagues, select teams, personal trainers, and out-of-state coaches bring new ideas and approaches, which can be both a blessing and a curse. While innovation is necessary for growth, these external entities often prioritize individual success over team cohesion, exacerbating the entitlement mentality and ultimately being fueled by someone's desire to make money off of youth sports.

Youth football and select teams, for instance, sometimes create unrealistic expectations for young athletes. They are groomed to believe that they are destined for greatness, fostering a sense of entitlement that can be detrimental when they face real competition. Personal trainers and outside coaches, though beneficial in some respects, may not always align with the values and goals of the high school programs, leading to conflicting agendas.

The question then arises: How can we preserve the greatness of high school football in the face of these challenges? The answer lies in returning to the core values that once defined the sport. Coaches, players, and administrators must recommit to the principles of hard work, loyalty, and resilience. They must understand that there will always be times when one must fight—when rolling up one's sleeves and getting to work is the only path to success.

Coaches need to instill loyalty and commitment in their players, reinforcing the importance of team over self. Players must be encouraged to embrace challenges and see adversity as an opportunity for growth, not an obstacle to avoid. District leadership should prioritize stability and the long-term development of coaches, creating an environment where programs can thrive, athletes can grow holistically, and coaches can see a clear path for their own growth as leaders within a district. Parents, too, have a role to play in this improvement. Trust us to coach your children fiercely. We promise to treat them as if they were our own. Watch us, hold us to our word.

The true greatness of high school football lies in its power to challenge entitlement and counter the growing softness of society. By fostering grit, determination, and loyalty, we can preserve the sport as a cornerstone of character development and competitive excellence. Now is the time for everyone involved to step up, commit to these values, and stand firm in what we know to be right.

COACH'S REFLECTION:

As we consider the challenges facing high school football today, let's take a moment to reflect.

- How can we better instill resilience and a strong work ethic in our players?
- In what ways can we cultivate a team-first mentality that prioritizes loyalty and commitment?
- What steps can we take to create a culture where challenges are embraced rather than avoided?
- How do our actions as coaches influence the overall mindset of our athletes?
- Are we, as leaders, doing enough to promote stability and long-term development within our programs?

These questions are designed to provoke thought and inspire meaningful conversations about the future of high school football.

CHAPTER 7

DEVELOPING COACHES, ANALYTICS, AND CONSERVATION

DEVELOPING TODAY'S COACHES

Coaches are masters of preparation and adaptation. For a true coach, there's nothing more rewarding than helping a player execute their assignments on a Friday night, knowing that many others would not have been able to guide that player to accomplish what they are doing on the field. Coaches thrive on teaching execution and precision because we understand that if a player can perform their role better than their opponent, the team will succeed.

Execution, however, is only half the formula. Effort is equally crucial. Exceptional effort on every play, every assignment, and every moment on the field is what elevates players to the next level. For coaches, the two fundamental measures of success, regardless of the sport, are execution and effort. Master these, and not only do you position yourself for victory on the field, but you also build lasting habits for success in the classroom, the workplace, and life itself.

That said, while coaches excel at accommodating and preparing their players, we must recognize that once Friday night arrives, those accommodations fall away. Winning comes down to which team can execute and think strategically best under pressure. Just like in life, whether you are interviewing for a big job or applying for your first mortgage, it is the smartest, most prepared, and most determined individuals who rise to the top.

After eight years away from education, I recently earned my special education certification in Texas to return to teaching and coaching football. During my time away, I dedicated myself to developing WARDBORD, a software platform for football coaches created to bridge the gap between traditional coaching methods and the way modern learners engage with information today.

When I was offered a position as a special education teacher and coach, I was not yet certified in special education. I took on the challenge, studied intensely for ten days, and earned my certification in record time. What truly surprised me was how much of what is expected of special education teachers mirrors the strategies and methods I had spent years researching. Approaches that modern learners need to thrive regardless of their learning abilities.

Here is the key takeaway: the principles that special education teachers are trained to understand and apply should not be reserved for just one group of students. These strategies should be foundational for all educators, no matter the subject or classroom. In fact, I would argue that every teacher would benefit from special education certification because it deepens their understanding of how students learn. Rather than prioritizing content knowledge above all else, our education system should focus on equipping teachers with the skills to connect with students, understand diverse learning needs, and build meaningful relationships that foster growth.

Of course, knowing your content is important. But as the world evolves, with artificial intelligence, instant access to information, and the rapid flow of knowledge, mastering teaching strategies and relationship-building will only grow in importance. As educators, we must adapt to this changing landscape. The reality is that much of the content knowledge future students acquire will not come directly from us. It will come from third-party sources, technology, and self-directed learning. Maybe that is not such a bad thing. What would be truly unfortunate is if we failed to adapt and did not do everything in our power to prepare young minds to navigate and excel in the world they will inherit.

The best coaches I have observed, and the most successful ones I have worked with, all understand this truth: the X's and O's, the technical content of the game, are secondary to the relationships they build and the character they instill in their players. Yes, they win football games, but their real legacy lies in the lives they have impacted. Great coaches are not just experts in strategy; they are leaders who prioritize connection, growth, and mentorship above all else.

As educators and coaches, our mission is clear: to focus on building individuals first. Content comes second. If we can embrace this mindset, we can truly unlock the potential of the young minds we are privileged to guide.

Developing coaches today demands an intentional approach. We must focus not only on coaching fundamentals but also on effectively connecting with players and understanding how they learn in today's world. The best coaches grasp the art of teaching, developing players physically and emotionally, and being organized both on and off the field. They are excellent communicators, often acting as psychologists and case managers to players and parents. They are innovative and constantly seek better ways for their players to learn. The more we empower players to learn, the more they will grow—but current learning styles are not always intuitive for many coaches. The landscape has shifted rapidly, and coaching practices must evolve to keep pace.

The art of developing coaches looks very different today. However, we often rely on surface-level efforts such as generic leadership books or cliché posters about character development. While these tools may be convenient, they fall short of truly preparing coaches. Instead, we should take a more thoughtful approach, helping new coaches master teaching strategies similar to those used by special education professionals, strategies tailored to meet diverse learning needs and styles.

In Chapter 10, I revisit the relationship between how players learn and how coaches teach. These two elements go hand in hand and are integral to building effective coaching methods. To truly prepare coaches for success, we must move beyond the basics of leadership and focus on fostering a deeper understanding of teaching, learning, and connection. This holistic development is the foundation of what real leadership in coaching should be.

Leadership is often misunderstood. It is not just about being loud, commanding attention, or knowing how to get a team to listen. True leadership runs deeper. It is timeless, disciplined, and multifaceted. It requires organization, strong communication, compassion, empathy, and a focus on helping others grow. Leadership is not simply about winning football games or earning respect through reputation. It is about doing the hard, often overlooked work, such as staying organized even when it is not a natural strength.

I will be the first to admit I am not perfect. In the past, I have made mistakes in how I handled certain situations with players, coaches, and parents. Looking back, I can see where I fell short, and if I had the chance, I would approach those moments differently today. However, I have worked hard to grow, becoming more patient, more understanding, and more reflective. That growth has given me perspective while also revealing deeper issues within youth sports. Favoritism, selfishness, and misplaced priorities are not just individual shortcomings; they are systemic problems that demand attention.

For those involved in hiring, especially school boards or anyone connected to them, I offer this advice: when interviewing a candidate for a head football coaching position, look beyond the surface. Pay close attention to how long they have remained in their current role and the longevity of their coaching staff. The coaches they have worked with, the team they have built, and the culture they have created often speak louder than their personal accolades. True leaders attract and retain great coaches, supporting their development until they are ready to advance in their own careers.

The best leaders are not driven by ego. They empower their staff, encourage autonomy, and cultivate a culture of innovation and collaboration. They understand that times are changing, players are changing, and relationships are changing, so they adapt. They are not afraid to challenge the status quo or try new approaches. These are the individuals who remain quietly confident yet enthusiastic in interviews. They show respect for their current administration, their staff, and the families connected to their programs. They also take the time to consider a new role thoughtfully rather than accepting it immediately. That is because they fully understand the weight of the responsibility they are stepping into.

When it comes to high-profile coaching jobs, especially in Texas, it is easy to assume they are all about the paycheck. But for the best coaches, that is not the case. These roles carry immense responsibility, and the influence of a great coach extends far beyond wins and losses. Coaches, both head coaches and their staff, shape the culture of schools and communities. Their impact is not limited to football but reaches across all sports programs, for both boys and girls.

Many coaches in smaller schools, who dedicate themselves tirelessly to their programs, are underpaid compared to the value they bring. Even the high-paying positions often fail to reflect the true worth of these leaders. Their influence runs deep, shaping not only athletes but the broader culture of schools and communities.

In the end, the coaches worth hiring are the ones who develop others. They build strong teams, foster growth, and create a lasting legacy of collaboration, innovation, and respect. Those are the leaders truly worth investing in. I may not be deeply familiar with everything our coaches' association does here in Texas, but one thing I do know is this: we have some incredible leaders with big hearts who are fully committed to advancing the coaching profession. One initiative that stands out is their mentorship program, which pairs aspiring head coaches with experienced coaches. Through regular meetings and mutual support, the program is designed to develop and nurture the next generation of leaders in our field. I think it is a fantastic concept, and I would be thrilled to one day contribute to this program, as I am incredibly passionate about our profession.

About three or four years ago, I attended the Lone Star Coaches Clinic to promote WARDBORD and had the privilege of meeting Coach Adam Harvey for the first time. What stood out most was not just his professionalism but his kindness, especially considering our initial interaction came with me on the other side of the table as a vendor. Many coaches do not realize what it feels like to be in that role, trying to share something valuable while most people avoid eye contact to dodge a sales pitch. Trust me, if you've ever been to a clinic where I am set up, I'm probably watching from 50 yards away, hoping you will stop and give me a chance.

When I met Coach Harvey, we did not focus much on what I was there to sell. Instead, we had a meaningful conversation about the coaching profession, its unique challenges, its importance, and, above all, the need to develop high-quality coaches. We discussed how critical it is for school districts to hire the right people and how, unfortunately, some districts get distracted by flashy resumes, advanced degrees, or dynamic interviews that do not always reveal a candidate's true abilities or values.

Even before Coach Harvey became a head coach, we talked about the idea of tracking and understanding a coach's "family tree." This concept, knowing where a coach comes from, who mentored them, and the philosophies they have inherited, could be invaluable in building a real network. It would allow us to understand not only the coach's history but also their values, leadership style, and the legacy they are contributing to the profession. At the time, this was just a dream we shared, but not long after, legendary coach D.W. Rutledge brought it to life.

I can't speak in detail about what Coach Rutledge has created, but I know his vision and intentions aligned with the very things Coach Harvey and I discussed. The coaching family tree concept adds a new level of credibility for aspiring coaches, highlighting traits and experiences that a resume alone may not capture. While being part of a great coaching tree does not guarantee someone is the perfect fit for a job, it sparks meaningful conversations in interviews that might not otherwise take place. It also fosters accountability, challenging us as coaches to reflect on the legacy we are building for the next generation.

Bad and even weak leaders often will not see the value in the coaching tree and may even dismiss it outright. Why? Because if they tried to create one, it would expose their shallow leadership, lacking both depth and substance. These are the coaches who leave no legacy because they fail to lead with purpose or passion. Their "trees" would have weak roots, much like their timid and uninspired approach to the profession.

In contrast, great coaches understand that success is not only about wins and losses but also about the impact they have on the people they lead and the future they help shape. That is the real game, and it is the one worth winning. Today's young coaches bring fresh perspectives and innovative strategies, yet they face unique challenges, including the pressure to meet high expectations both on and off the field. They are expected not only to produce winning teams but also to mentor young athletes through personal and professional challenges. Balancing these dual responsibilities can be daunting, especially in a world full of modern distractions.

This raises an important question: how can we intentionally focus on leadership development in an environment that often pulls attention in every direction? With limited time, there is a real risk of reducing leadership development to a box-ticking exercise, an uninspiring obligation rather than a meaningful pursuit. Achieving genuine leadership development that leaves a lasting impact on our profession requires both courage and insight. This is not a criticism of current leaders, but it is possible that their past experiences limit their ability to see the world through the eyes of today's and tomorrow's coaches. Leadership evolves with time, but its core values and purpose must remain consistent.

Legendary, seasoned coaches must take the lead in guiding the evolution of our profession, but they cannot do it alone. Collaboration with those who are focused on the future and committed to bridging generational divides is essential. These divides are real, whether we acknowledge them or not. They are not inherently negative, nor do they signal a decline in our profession, but if ignored, they risk eroding the core values that hold us together. To secure a thriving future, we must deliberately bridge these gaps with a shared commitment to growth and progress.

True leadership extends far beyond administrative tasks. It is about inspiring others, fostering growth, and leaving a lasting impact on individuals and teams. Leadership is not simply writing practice schedules or deciding when to call a timeout. Creative leadership empowers and develops high-performing coaches, while poor leadership produces complacency and followers. Given our history, the current challenges, and the ever-changing global sports landscape, deliberate leadership development has never been more critical. The next generation of leaders will grow out of the coaching legacies being built today, creating a ripple effect that will shape the lives of countless young people for years to come.

At 41, I often reflect on my journey as a coach and the pivotal moments that have shaped my philosophy, both within the profession and beyond. One particularly subtle yet impactful moment involved Coach Tony Castillo, who embodied the true spirit of camaraderie in coaching.

During my second year as a high school coach, my defensive line was running one-on-one drills against his offensive line, and his players were consistently outperforming mine. Tony could have easily gloated, something I admit I have been guilty of when on the winning side, but he did not. Instead, he took the time to teach me the push-pull drill, a technique my players clearly needed to master. Over the following practices and weeks, I integrated it into my coaching, and the results were transformative. That simple act of mentorship revealed the power of shared knowledge and peer support in a profession where collaboration can make all the difference.

Coming off a season in a far more chaotic coaching environment, Tony's kindness and willingness to help were invaluable. He did not see a rival coach; he saw a young coach who could benefit from guidance. His gesture may have been small, but its impact was enduring. He may not even remember it, but I certainly do.

I share this story not because it is extraordinary, but because it highlights the profound influence of small, thoughtful gestures in shaping future coaches. It often takes so little to make a lasting difference.

Looking back, it is almost laughable how fundamental the push-pull drill is. Something every defensive line coach knows intimately. But at that point in my career, I was coaching with a player's mindset, focusing on drills for the sake of drills rather than teaching my players how those drills applied to their positions. I was not intentional in aligning my coaching techniques with the specific demands of the game. Tony's mentorship helped me realize that coaching is not just about running drills; it's about teaching, guiding, and helping players and coaches truly understand their craft. That lesson has stayed with me ever since.

THE OVER-RELIANCE ON ANALYTICS IN HIGH SCHOOL FOOTBALL COACHING

Another crucial aspect of being a courageous coach is outlining a clear path for oneself and others. This involves setting bold goals and understanding the broader purpose behind them. In coaching, the goal might be to win, but the purpose is to build a cohesive team and instill a love for the sport. By separating goals from purposes, courageous coaches maintain clarity and discipline, ensuring their actions align with their broader mission.

In competition, while the objective is to win, the true purpose often lies in challenging oneself and fostering personal growth. Similarly, on social media, boosting visibility is the goal, but the deeper intention is to connect with a broader community and share valuable insights. Understanding these distinctions helps courageous coaches refine their focus and lead with intention, ensuring every effort aligns with a greater purpose. This clarity is crucial for young coaches striving to make a lasting impact on their players, both on and off the field.

As we look for ways to enhance player performance on the field, it is important to acknowledge the recent transformations in high school football brought about by data analytics. Metrics and statistics have become central to game preparation and practice planning, pushing many coaches to adjust their strategies, but an overreliance on analytics can diminish the value of direct feedback and player evaluations, both of which are vital to the growth of young athletes. Striking the right balance between analytics, personal development, and community engagement enables coaches to create a lasting and meaningful legacy.

THE YOUNGER GENERATION OF COACHES AND ANALYTICS

The rise of younger coaches in high school football has been a driving force behind the increased use of analytics in the sport. Recent surveys show that the average age of high school coaches has dropped, with many now in their late 20s to early 30s. These younger coaches, often tech-savvy and data-driven, are more likely to view analytics as a powerful decision-making tool.

According to a study by Recruiting Analytics, effectively applying tracking data can improve a coach's success rate by up to three times. This has fueled a growing dependence on analytics, often treated as a nearly infallible guide. Yet this reliance can sometimes overshadow the value of personalized feedback and hands-on coaching, both of which are essential to the holistic development of student-athletes. It is important to remember that, in critical moments, analytics often take a backseat. When the game is on the line, courage and instinct tend to outweigh data-packed call sheets and opponent breakdowns. In those moments, heart and intuition lead the way.

Coaching education should emphasize not only how to use analytics but also how to identify which metrics truly add value and which create unnecessary work. Too often, the inefficiencies of certain tools and data sets are overlooked, resources that demand significant time without delivering meaningful benefits to the team. Coaches must learn to protect their time, maximize resources, and evaluate their players' capacity to process and apply analytical insights effectively.

It is also worth acknowledging that, as coaches, we sometimes try to do too much. We overload players with excessive data and strategies, forgetting they have lives beyond the field. By overwhelming them with information they cannot realistically absorb or implement, we risk complicating the game unnecessarily. As much as football matters, it is not the only thing in their world. Striking the right balance, using analytics where it counts while respecting the broader context of our players' lives, is essential. More often than not, simplicity and focus win the day.

GENERATION Z ATHLETES AND THEIR LEARNING STYLES

Today's high school football players are part of Generation Z, a group defined by its unique learning styles and deep connection with technology. These athletes favor quick, easily digestible information and are highly skilled at using digital tools. With a strong sense of independence, many have developed self-taught habits, often turning to online resources for knowledge.

Despite their tech-savvy nature, Generation Z athletes thrive on direct and personalized feedback. Studies show they respond best to clear, concise communication and value understanding the "why" behind their training and strategies. They excel in environments where coaches consistently provide constructive advice, balancing recognition of their strengths with actionable insights for improvement.

While their learning preferences are discussed more thoroughly in Chapter 10, it is important to acknowledge the impact of growing up in a world dominated by technology. These athletes have had constant access to smartphones, tablets, and the internet, shaping how they learn and make decisions. They have never known a life without instant access to information, which has made them habitual questioners. With a quick online search, they seek answers, accurate or not, and this habit profoundly influences the way they learn and form opinions.

A common challenge coaches face with this generation stems from misunderstandings about their mindset. For example, after a victory, we might recognize that the team's performance fell short of what is required for long-term success. Perhaps assignments were missed, or the effort was not strong enough to secure critical wins in the future. Yet because the scoreboard shows a win, players may not immediately grasp the disconnect. It is easy to assume they are being careless, entitled, or complacent when, in reality, words alone often fail to resonate.

The best way to bridge this gap is by presenting players with concrete data that clearly illustrates where they fell short. For too long, we have overlooked this approach, relying instead on analytics and trends from flashy video platforms. While such tools can be useful, they often fail to provide what players need most: clear, factual insights about their own performance in a way they can fully understand. Be honest with them. Do not sugarcoat the message or bury it in unnecessary complexity. Players need authentic, straightforward feedback if they are to grow.

THE PSYCHOLOGICAL COMFORT OF ANALYTICS

For many coaches, analytics provide a sense of reassurance. The objectivity of data offers a solid foundation for decision-making, reducing the uncertainty and subjective bias often associated with traditional coaching methods. Real-time metrics and insights give coaches a feeling of control and confidence in their strategies.

However, this reliance on analytics can sometimes overshadow other critical aspects of coaching. The subtleties of player behavior, team dynamics, and individual psychological states often fall outside the scope of raw data. These elements require a coach's intuition, experience, and interpersonal skills, qualities that no algorithm can replicate.

THE VALUE OF FEEDBACK

While analytics can be an invaluable tool, they must never replace the cornerstone of coaching: constructive feedback. Feedback is essential to player development, especially for young athletes. It helps them understand their performance, track progress, and identify areas for improvement. More importantly, it shows them that growth is not defined only by statistics, which may not always capture their true contribution to the team.

Feedback also nurtures a growth mindset, encouraging athletes to see challenges as opportunities rather than setbacks. It strengthens trust and rapport between coaches and players, creating an environment where athletes feel valued and supported. By delivering clear, actionable feedback, coaches empower players to take ownership of their development.

This process is far more effective than simply encouraging players to watch more game film, a common but often unproductive practice. Many players lack the skills to analyze film critically, focusing only on their own highlights without gaining meaningful insights. This approach fails to teach them how to contribute meaningfully to the larger goal of winning.

Consider this: coaches frequently demand more from players than any school subject, yet we often provide them with far less preparation material for independent study. This discrepancy is counterproductive. Coaches should lean on the experience of veteran colleagues, those who come from an era where assessing players and delivering detailed, play-by-play feedback was a primary focus, unburdened by today's complex analytics.

At its core, football strategy remains simple: every play is designed to either score points or stop the opponent. Success hinges on all eleven players executing their assignments within a well-crafted plan. Perhaps it is time to blend the wisdom of "old-school" coaching with modern innovations, drawing on the expertise of seasoned coaches who excelled in areas like detailed player evaluations and personalized feedback.

CONSERVATION IN COACHING

Reflecting on the coaching profession, I often find myself considering the parallels between coaching and wildlife conservation. I once listened to a podcast about wildlife conservation in Texas, a subject that resonated deeply with me. The representative spoke about their mission to protect and preserve ecosystems, and it struck me how rarely we talk about conserving our own profession, protecting its integrity and ensuring its future.

Curious, I looked up the definition of conservation. According to the dictionary conservation is "the planned management of something to prevent exploitation, destruction, or neglect". This definition feels profoundly relevant to coaching. It is not only about innovation or adaptation; it is about preserving the core values and practices that define our profession. As coaching evolves, we must hold on to the principles that inspired us to pursue this path in the first place. These are the same principles that would make the legendary coaches who once guided us proud.

At its best, coaching combines data-driven insights with the timeless art of teaching, mentoring, and leading. By conserving these values, we not only honor the legacy of our profession but also ensure that the next generation of coaches inherits a rich and meaningful tradition. The challenge is to embrace innovation while remaining rooted in what truly matters, striking a balance between forward-thinking strategies and the methods that have stood the test of time.

THE RISKS OF OVERRELIANCE ON ANALYTICS IN COACHING

While analytics has become an essential tool in modern sports, relying too heavily on data can create serious drawbacks for both players and coaches. Leaning too heavily on analytics narrows attention to what can be measured, often sidelining critical aspects of development such as character, teamwork, and mental resilience. Players risk feeling depersonalized, reduced to statistics rather than recognized as individuals with unique talents and needs.

Excessive emphasis on analytics can also stifle creativity and intuition, qualities vital for both players and coaches. Football, at its core, is a dynamic and unpredictable game that demands quick thinking, adaptability, and spontaneity. When strategies become too rigid and data-driven, they can break down in the fluid, high-pressure environment of live competition. Overreliance on numbers can also shift accountability away from effort and execution, diminishing the value of determination and grit, qualities that championship-level teams consistently prioritize.

To succeed, modern coaching must find balance: analytics should support, not replace, the traditional methods of mentorship and feedback. This is particularly important with Generation Z athletes, who often thrive when given both data-driven insights and meaningful human connection. The future of coaching lies in blending the precision of analytics with the personal touch, ensuring that metrics enhance the game without eroding its core values.

Developing the next generation of coaches will require strong leadership, clear goals, and a commitment to principles that define great coaching. By fostering mentorship, encouraging innovation, and upholding the timeless values of sportsmanship and growth, we can empower young coaches to navigate the complexities of modern athletics. In doing so, we ensure that the legacy of sports endures not just as a test of skill, but as a platform for character, teamwork, and resilience.

COACH'S REFLECTION:

Take a moment to reflect on how courage influences your leadership and coaching practices. Use these prompts to guide your thoughts:

- How do you currently display courage in challenging coaching situations?

- How does showing courage help you build stronger trust and respect with your team?

- Can you recall a time when courage helped you uphold your values during a tough decision? What was the impact?

- How can you inspire your team to step beyond their comfort zones and embrace growth?

- Are there fears—such as fear of failure or resistance to change—holding you back as a coach? What steps can you take to overcome these fears?

Courage is a vital quality in coaching in that it enables leaders to face challenges, uphold integrity, and inspire growth. By reflecting on these questions, you can deepen your understanding of how courage shapes your leadership and foster an environment where both you and your team can thrive.

CHAPTER 8

FOUNDATIONS, SALARIES, PATIENCE, RETENTION, AND MOTIVE

High school football coaches are often seen as pillars of strength and strategy on the field, but the journey to becoming the coach they aspire to be requires immense patience, perseverance, and faith. It is a slow, deliberate process, much like nurturing a dream that unfolds over time, shaped by experience, mentorship, and personal growth.

In Chapter 2, I touched on "aspirational marketing" and how it perpetuates the idea that we are never enough, subtly conditioning many of us to see ourselves in a diminished light. This constant narrative not only impacts young players but also affects us as coaches. While we may be more aware of these pressures than our players, we are not immune to the relentless self-doubt and negative reminders that surround us every day.

THE COACHING TREE: A PATHWAY TO GROWTH AND CONFIDENCE

Becoming a great coach is not just about mastering X's and O's, but about finding your place within a coaching tree that embodies integrity and excellence. A coaching tree is more than a network; it is a nurturing ecosystem where young coaches can learn, grow, and develop into leaders. It provides guidance not just on the technicalities of the game, but also on essential values like patience, resilience, and leadership. Being part of a great coaching tree offers young coaches a sense of belonging and purpose within the profession. It builds confidence and provides a clear path to growth and success. As a member of a coaching lineage, you are reminded that you are part of something larger, something that supports you as you develop and prepare for pivotal roles, such as landing your first coordinator position.

This sense of lineage is critical in an era where young athletes, and even young coaches, are conditioned to seek instant answers. Modern learners often turn to the internet for quick solutions, regardless of their accuracy. As coaches, we frequently have to prove things to our players, showing them why their performance fell short or how they can improve. The same principle applies to young coaches. They also need proof, one that patience, trust in the process, and doing things the right way will pay off in the long run.

Documenting and sharing your coaching lineage is an effective way to instill confidence in young coaches. It shows them that their efforts are not in vain and that patience and dedication will lead to success. By embracing the lessons passed down through the coaching tree, they not only grow into their roles but also gain the privilege of mentoring the next generation, continuing the cycle of excellence and integrity.

Ultimately, the coaching journey is a testament to the values we instill in our players: perseverance, teamwork, and unwavering commitment to growth. And just like our players, we must remember that the process is worth its weight in gold.

BEYOND THE MONEY: A DEEPER PURPOSE

In today's world, discussions about the highest-paid coaches and the rise of NIL (Name, Image, and Likeness) money dominate social media feeds. Some of you may have explored these topics before, while others may not pay them much attention. Regardless, it is worth noting that the top-paid high school football coaches in Texas earn significantly more than the statewide average. While the **average salary** for a Texas high school head football coach sits around **$98,668**, those leading elite programs often earn **between $135,000 and $180,000** annually. These higher salaries tend to be concentrated in schools with rich football traditions, strong community support, and consistent playoff success.

This pay disparity underscores the immense value placed on leadership and sustained excellence in these programs. Schools are willing to invest heavily in coaching talent to maintain their competitive edge, a reflection of the deep ties between football and community identity in Texas.

To outsiders unfamiliar with the generational impact of these roles, such salaries may seem excessive or even unfair, especially in the context of education. But as someone who has been immersed in this world, I can confidently say these coaches are not paid enough. And this extends beyond head coaches to include coordinators and position coaches as well.

This leads to a broader perspective on how we view compensation, inspired by Dan Pallotta's thought-provoking TED Talk. I watched it a few years ago, and it completely shifted how I perceive the nonprofit sector and, by extension, professions like coaching. Society often undervalues roles that leave a lasting impact on communities. While there are exceptions, I encourage you to consider a different lens, one that recognizes the transformative influence these coaches have on young athletes, their schools, and their communities.

It is time to rethink how we view high school coaching salaries and the value these individuals bring to the table. They are more than coaches; they are leaders, mentors, and builders of future generations.

In his compelling TED Talk, Dan Pallotta challenges society's outdated approach to judging nonprofit leaders. He highlights how we penalize those striving to make a difference by clinging to misguided expectations about money:

"We let people make millions selling violent video games, but we don't want the head of a hunger charity to earn more than a school principal."

This belief, that doing good must require personal sacrifice, echoes a familiar debate over the high salaries of high school football coaches. In states like Texas, top coaches can earn between $150,000 and $180,000, sparking criticism rooted in emotional optics: "It's just high school football," or "Teachers make far less." But these arguments often oversimplify the profound impact elite coaches have, not just on wins and scholarships, but on shaping **entire school cultures and communities.**

Pallotta explains that undervaluing leadership in the nonprofit sector leads to devastating consequences:

"If you can get a $400,000 salary changing the world at Apple, but only $84,000 trying to cure hunger, we're creating a disincentive for smart people to tackle hard problems."

The same principle applies to high school coaches. When we undervalue those who mentor **more than 100 athletes**, build programs from the ground up, instill discipline, and step in as father figures for kids with no other role models, we are not debating dollars. We are **dismissing transformational leadership**.

Head coaches often function more like CEOs than teachers. Their responsibilities extend far beyond the field and include:

- Player development and safety
- Character-building and life-skills education
- Staffing and managing personnel
- Communicating with parents
- Media relations and public perception

- College recruitment pipelines
- Logistics, data analysis, and maintaining team morale

Yet because their successes are not measured in test scores, their salaries are frequently viewed as excessive. As Pallotta would argue, **we are asking the wrong question.** The issue is not whether someone earns six figures, but whether they deliver six-figure results in the lives they transform, the opportunities they create, and the programs they build.

"We confuse morality with frugality. We're judging how little people spend rather than how much they accomplish."

In both nonprofit leadership and high school coaching, the message is clear: **Big impact requires bold investment**. It is time to stop punishing effectiveness simply because it comes with a paycheck.

You might be wondering why I went off on a tangent about what coaches get paid. Let me clarify: this is not an argument for higher salaries, but rather a reflection on the conversations I know are happening in every community. You have likely heard them too, at halftime, by the concession stands, or during games when people say, "We should be winning." Coaching, at its core, is not about the paycheck. It is about the profound impact we have on young athletes, the lessons we instill, and the personal growth we experience along the way. The true rewards of coaching come from the relationships we build, the lives we touch, and the legacy we leave behind.

That being said, let's face reality. If we live in a world that places sports on such a high pedestal, we need to acknowledge a hard truth: you get what you pay for. What the articles and online discussions rarely mention are the sacrifices coaches make behind the scenes. The family events, vacations, milestones, firsts, lasts, and everything in between that coaches miss because they are busy doing what is right for someone else's kids.

What is often overlooked is the toll this takes on their own families, the missed moments, the unspoken neglect, and sometimes the lasting damage. Coaches' families need them just as much as the players do, and navigating these demands is no small feat. It requires understanding, patience, and a strong sense of community. Coaches, teachers, and administrators must work together to foster an environment that supports everyone involved. This collaboration is essential not only to the success of players, but also to the well-being of the families and individuals who dedicate their lives to this demanding profession.

Lately, there's been a growing conversation among coaches about the importance of prioritizing family. In his book *Swagger*, legendary coach Jimmy Johnson reflects on his career with a sense of regret, wishing he had been more present for his family during pivotal moments. Johnson shares deeply personal stories, including the challenges his son faced with alcoholism and the profound impact it had on him as both a father and a coach.

He candidly admits that the relentless demands of his career often kept him away during times when his family needed him most. His son's struggle with addiction became a wake-up call, forcing Johnson to confront the emotional consequences of his absence. The experience left a lasting impression, highlighting the critical importance of balancing professional commitments with being present for loved ones.

Thankfully, this story has a hopeful ending. Johnson's son, Chad J. Johnson, turned his journey into a powerful purpose, founding Tranquil Shores in 2009, a leading adult rehab and addiction recovery center specializing in integrative treatment. While it was a long and difficult road, it is a testament to resilience and the strength of familial bonds.

Stories like this serve as a reminder of why protecting and prioritizing our families is essential, even in the face of demanding careers. They underscore the profound value of being present for those who matter most. Bruce Arians has made his stance on work-life balance clear: he would fire any coach who skips their child's recital or Little League game. His perspective underscores the irreplaceable value of family moments and the importance of prioritizing them, even in demanding careers like coaching.

Tony Dungy echoes this sentiment, emphasizing that finding harmony between work and family is not only essential for a fulfilling life but also for longevity in coaching. His insights remind us that true success lies in balancing professional achievements with meaningful personal relationships.

This philosophy is not limited to a few notable names. A quick search for "head football coaches on family" will reveal countless quotes and stories from leaders in the field who reflect on the dynamics of a coaching family, their proudest moments, and often, their regrets. For any coach reading this, I urge you to pay close attention the next time you attend a coaching clinic. When you are sitting in that room, listening to a legendary or highly successful coach discuss their schemes, team culture, and lessons learned over the years, notice how many of them end their talks by shifting focus to family.

In my experience attending coaching clinics as a vendor over the past five years, I have observed a consistent pattern. When these coaches speak about family, there is a noticeable change in their tone, expressions, and demeanor. They often conclude with a heartfelt message such as, "Take care of your family first." Sometimes it is brief, but their passion is unmistakable. You can see it in their eyes, a conviction that family must come first. It is a look that says they are willing to fight for this truth, and anyone who disagrees is not aligned with the values of a true coach.

As coaches, we have an obligation to prioritize our families. That means being more productive, efficient, and intentional with our time. It also means fostering an open environment in our coaching offices, one where we don't just say "It's okay to leave for your kid's event," but truly mean it. Early in my coaching career, before I had kids, I might have judged a coach for walking out of the office for a family commitment. If I had been a parent back then, I probably would have missed many important moments.

As a parent and coach, my perspective has completely shifted. I'll leave the office instantly for my kids' events, yet still ensure everything gets done. My team and players will be ready to compete, practice, and succeed on the field. And if you are the kind of coach who stays at the office late, thinking that makes you the ultimate "ball coach," I can promise you this: I'll find time for my family and still be prepared to beat you on gameday. That's how an "Armageddon Coach" does things.

Preparation and success are critical, but so is making it clear to your staff that family comes first. When you give your coaches permission to step away, make sure they know you mean it 100 percent. They will respect you more as a leader, and they will still get their responsibilities handled in time for Monday's practice. Guaranteed.

THE GIFT OF PATIENCE

Patience is the cornerstone of great coaching. It is about recognizing that success is a journey, not a sprint, and that mistakes are stepping stones toward growth. Coaches must extend patience not only to their players but also to themselves as they navigate challenges on and off the field. This patience allows for a deeper understanding of their own strengths and weaknesses, insights that shape the most successful coaches. The best coaches know their strengths and, more importantly, understand their areas for growth.

As you grow into your role as a football coach, you will discover that experience and exposure to other great leaders teach you something invaluable. Legendary coaches have an extraordinary ability to adapt. They become whatever their team needs them to be, even if it means stepping outside of their comfort zone. While they naturally lean on their strengths from day to day, in critical moments they transform to meet the unique demands of their team. This evolution does not happen overnight. It takes time, patience, and the willingness to stay in one place long enough to see it through.

At its core, coaching is an act of love. Love for the game, for the players, and for the process. This love gives us the strength to endure what can often be a challenging path. The expectations placed on coaches and educators today can feel unrelenting, but the rewards far outweigh the sacrifices. Coaching is a journey filled with highs and lows, an emotional roller coaster where, at some point, you are almost guaranteed to face setbacks, including the possibility of being let go.

I will be the first to admit that not every coaching dismissal comes from bad intentions or an "evil" school board member. Sometimes a school or community simply needs change, a fresh perspective to revitalize its culture. While this change can be painful, it is often necessary. It reminds me of a quote by G. Michael Hopf: *"Hard times create strong men, strong men create good times, good times create weak men, and weak men create hard times."*

I first heard this quote from Coach Aaron McKie, former NBA player and current basketball coach, during a memorial for his mentor, John Chaney. In his speech, McKie reflected on the cycles of life, resilience, and the lessons he learned from Coach Chaney. He spoke about going from walking to driving luxury cars and back again, illustrating the inevitable ups and downs of life. His words serve as a powerful reminder to stay grounded and never grow complacent, no matter where you are in your journey.

As coaches, it is easy to become impatient, to forget the lessons that shaped us, and to lose sight of what truly matters. Complacency dulls our edge. But at the end of the day, success begins with doing right by our players. Stay patient, stay committed, and remember that love and grace are the foundation of this long and meaningful journey.

LEARNING FROM THE PAST

Reflecting on Coach McKie's speech reminds me of the importance of remembering "that coach" who inspired us back in the day. Think about the qualities that made them impactful: their patience, their approachability, and their ability to balance football with life lessons.

Many young coaches today may not even realize what they need until they see it modeled by seasoned mentors.

Holistic development is essential for creating not only great coaches but also well-rounded individuals. Think about the coaches who shaped you: their consistency, their presence throughout your high school years, and the way they welcomed you into their families. They showed patience in ways we did not fully understand at the time, and that patience was a form of grace. It did not just sharpen our skills on the field; it shaped our character off it. Those lessons stay with us forever.

Creating a supportive environment extends far beyond the game of football. It is about building a sense of community and belonging. It means welcoming players, young coaches, and their families into your life, showing them what love, family, and consistency look like through real, meaningful experiences. I will never forget my defensive line coach from high school, Coach Andy Cellars, who once hosted a simple spaghetti dinner at his home for our position group. Small gestures like this leave a lasting impact, strengthening relationships and showing others that they are valued, that our bond goes deeper than just the sport.

I will delve further into Coach Cellars in the next chapter, but it is important to highlight a fundamental truth: as mentors, we bear the responsibility to offer players and young coaches the same kindness, patience, and support our own mentors once extended to us. Show them grace, provide guidance, and encourage their growth, all while valuing their fresh perspectives and energy. Coaching is about far more than winning games. It is about shaping individuals, building meaningful connections, and creating a legacy that transcends the playing field.

THE CHALLENGE OF RETAINING COACHES

The world of high school football coaching today is filled with challenges. Coaches often move from one job to another, searching for something that seems just out of reach with a sense of purpose and belonging that transcends a paycheck. For Texas high school football coaches, a close-knit fraternity, losing one's place in this community can happen all too easily. To address this issue, we must return to the roots of why we chose this path: to change lives and make a lasting difference.

In the corporate world, leaders have recognized that retaining employees requires more than competitive salaries. While compensation matters, it is often about fostering a culture that encourages a sense of purpose and provides clarity through strong leadership. Clear expectations, a shared vision, and a supportive environment can boost job satisfaction and strengthen loyalty. The same principles apply to coaching.

As coaches, it is also critical to find fulfillment beyond the field. While personal happiness is our responsibility, the schools and districts we work for play a significant role in shaping an environment where we can thrive personally and professionally. By focusing on purpose, community, and well-being, we can create a culture that sustains not just our passion for coaching, but also the lives of the players we are privileged to guide.

REDISCOVERING THE PURPOSE OF COACHING

Understanding why we coach is vital. While motivations may differ, the core purpose remains constant. As Daniel H. Pink explains in his book *Drive*, intrinsic motivation driven by autonomy, mastery, and purpose-far surpasses the influence of external rewards or recognition. Many of us chose to become coaches because someone once transformed our lives, inspiring us to pay it forward to the next generation. Great coaches are often skilled at commanding attention when necessary, but their drive does not stem from seeking the spotlight or public praise. Instead, they are fueled by a deeper purpose, focused on making a meaningful impact rather than conforming to external expectations or seeking validation.

Pink's framework highlights that individuals perform their best when they feel ownership over their work, are encouraged to develop their skills, and understand the broader purpose behind their actions. As coaches, we must embrace this mindset. We are not just teaching plays or strategies; we are equipping our players with life lessons they will carry long after they leave the field.

Staying true to this intrinsic drive can be challenging, especially in a profession where external pressures and public perceptions often dominate. Great coaching is not about theatrics on the sidelines, yelling, throwing clipboards, or grabbing facemasks to put on a show for the crowd. These displays do not define a coach's ability. As a more experienced coach, I have learned that being loud is not what makes you effective. The best coaches focus on what truly matters: teaching, mentoring, and making an impact.

To fans, administrators, and school board members watching from the stands, remember this: the loudest voices do not always have the most meaningful things to say. A coach's value lies not in sideline behavior but in the ability to inspire, guide, and transform players' lives. We must work together to attract and retain coaches who are motivated by these deeper principles, those who move the needle not just in football, but in life.

THE JOURNEY OF COACHING

Becoming the coach you aspire to be is a process that requires patience, perseverance, and personal growth. Embrace the beauty of the journey, stay grounded in your purpose, and never lose sight of the incredible impact you have on young lives.

At the same time, let us not forget the families behind every coach. Supporting coaches, especially those with young children, is crucial, as the demands of this profession can be overwhelming. By fostering a community that values balance, purpose, and well-being, we can create an environment where both our teams and families thrive.

In the end, coaching is about more than wins and losses. It is about shaping character, building community, and creating a legacy. Let us strive to nurture a culture where coaches are empowered to lead with heart and motivated by the lasting difference they make. Together, we can ensure the future of coaching remains bright—for ourselves, for our players, and for the communities we serve.

COACH'S REFLECTION

As you think about your coaching journey, consider how the themes of this chapter resonate with your experience. Reflect on the following questions to gain deeper insight:

- What initially sparked your passion for coaching, and how has that motivation evolved as you've grown in your role?

- Are you managing to strike a healthy balance between your coaching duties and your personal life? What adjustments could help you find better harmony?

- How do you contribute to building a supportive network for fellow coaches, particularly those managing family responsibilities?

- In what ways are you creating a positive, inclusive, and motivating environment for your team?

- What methods do you use to assess the impact you are making on the lives of the young people you work with?

- Are you prioritizing your own mental and emotional health as you guide and mentor others?

Taking time to reflect on these questions can help you align your coaching approach with your values and goals, address any challenges, and strengthen your commitment to personal growth and the development of those you coach.

CHAPTER 9

THE BATTLE AGAINST FATHERLESSNESS

My old defensive line coach, Andy Cellars, spent eleven years on the football field before deciding to transition into administration. I ran into him during a staff development day just before the start of the 2025 school year. On a whim, I asked what he remembered most from those evenings when he invited us into his home for spaghetti dinners after practice. I did not mention that I was gathering material for this part of the book; I simply wanted to hear his reflections.

What he shared became the perfect segue into this chapter. He described those nights vividly: a crowded living room filled with players far too big for his furniture, laughter echoing off the walls, and the warmth of shared meals. Players would joke around, eat their fill, and even play with his kids in the living room, acting like big brothers on an ordinary weeknight. The scene felt like something straight out of an old "Andy Griffith" episode, with a wholesome family dinner followed by playtime.

Coach Cellars told me he never once hesitated to open his home to his players. He trusted their hearts, their goodness, and the way they cared for his family. Just like the Walkers, who I wrote about earlier in Chapter 3, Cellars extended his family to include his players because that is what great coaches do: they love harder than they coach.

But then, as he lingered on those joyful memories, his tone grew heavier. He wondered about the players who had gone on to face darker fates, the ones who ended up in prison after high school. He spoke of kids with hearts as big as Texas, kids who could light up a room, only to later find themselves confined behind concrete walls. Cellars questioned whether he could have done more to change their paths, a sentiment I have heard echoed by countless coaches over the years. They have seen promising young men go from playing with toy cars on their living room floors to fighting battles they could not win, trapped in lives they never deserved.

It was this heartbreak, Cellars told me, that led him to leave coaching and move into school administration. He wanted to have a broader impact, to influence the system on a larger scale. Coaches are some of the most determined people I know, but they also understand when a play is not working and it is time to pivot. They know how to adapt, how to put their players in the best possible position to succeed. For Cellars, stepping into administration was his way of taking the fight beyond the field- to address the deeper, darker challenges that lie beneath the surface.

As I listened to him, I could not help but recall a quote I once heard Joe Rogan say. I am paraphrasing, but it went something like this: "I never knew how bad my parents were until I had my own kids. Then I thought, wow, this is how you're supposed to feel about your kids." In a podcast with Theo Von, Rogan explored the heartbreaking reality of fatherlessness in today's world. It is not just about the absence of a parent; it is about what that absence leaves behind. We are living in an era where this silent epidemic is shaping the lives of millions, and it is a truth that goes unspoken far too often.

Coach Cellars' story, along with the stories of so many coaches like him, reminds us that the impact of a mentor can be profound. But it also reminds us that the challenges we face in shaping young lives go far beyond the sidelines. They demand more from all of us if we are to truly make a difference.

Joe Rogan, one of the most prominent voices in modern media, has spoken openly about the absence of his father and how becoming a dad himself revealed what he had been missing. He described his childhood as emotionally detached, punctuated by brief and tumultuous encounters with a violent father. Reflecting on those early years, Rogan said, *"All my damage came from my real father before I was seven."*

It was not until he had children of his own that the true weight of his father's absence hit him. Raising his kids, being present, guiding them, and listening forced him to confront just how deeply his parents had failed him. In striving to become the kind of parent he never had, Rogan came to understand the profound void left behind.

This same dynamic quietly unfolds every day on practice fields and in locker rooms across the country. For many young athletes, their football coach becomes the closest thing to a father figure they will ever know. Coaches set expectations, hold players accountable, and show up consistently. Most importantly, they believe in these young men when no one else does. While Rogan found healing and purpose through fatherhood, thousands of young men find structure, discipline, and confidence through coaching. At its best, the coaching profession bridges generational gaps caused by emotional absence, one rep, one game plan, one impactful conversation at a time.

In his book *Fathered by God*, John Eldredge captures this truth, describing a world where "boys walk around in men's bodies." That idea resonates deeply. Without the steady presence of a father, many young men struggle to find their way into adulthood, lacking the mentorship, guidance, and unconditional support that a father traditionally provides. This absence leaves lasting scars, and the ripple effects often show up in society in troubling ways.

For countless young men, high school football becomes much more than a game; it becomes a lifeline. The football field offers structure, discipline, and a unique form of love that many have never experienced. Coaches step into the void as father figures, offering something that can change a young man's life: unconditional love and belief in his potential.

While much of this discussion revolves around fatherlessness, it is equally important to acknowledge the impact of emotionally absent parents, whether fathers or mothers who, despite being physically present, may unknowingly create trauma in their children's lives. Dr. Gabor Maté explains that trauma is not only about what happens to us but also *what fails to happen for us.* He writes, *"Children can be wounded in multiple ways: by bad things happening, yes, but also by good things not happening, such as their emotional needs for attunement not being met."*

Parents who are distracted, stressed, or emotionally unavailable may unintentionally leave their children feeling unseen and unsafe. This subtle form of trauma occurs when a child's emotional needs for connection and validation go unmet. As Maté emphasizes, *"Every human has a true, genuine, authentic self. Trauma is the disconnection from it."* When parents miss everyday opportunities to connect, children often lose touch with their authentic selves, adapting their behavior to gain approval or avoid rejection.

For many coaches, this is the true essence of their work. It is not about wins or trophies; it is about being that steady, unwavering presence. There is a special kind of joy in hearing a player say, "Hey, Coach," often just wanting to talk, whether it is about football or not. That simple gesture is a reminder of the profound influence coaches carry. The title "Coach" holds a weight and an honor that those in the profession guard closely.

At its core, coaching becomes a form of fatherhood for those who need it most. For these young men, the impact is life-changing, shaped through one practice, one conversation, and one moment of belief at a time.

Reflecting on my own journey, I have come to understand why coaching feels so deeply meaningful to me. Growing up, my coaches were the first men to show me unconditional love. No matter what happened on or off the field, they were there with guidance and support. While I was a fiery football player, proud of pushing my limits and testing my opponents, those who know me personally would likely describe me as straight-laced and well-behaved. The love my coaches provided left a lasting imprint, and I believe many of the young athletes we coach today experience the same. They feel that love, even if they cannot always articulate it or recognize it in the moment. Often, only with time and reflection do they fully grasp the significance of that bond.

For me, offering that same unconditional love to the next generation of players is what makes coaching so powerful. We care for these young men, and we are not afraid to show it or say it: we love them.

Many of us describe coaching as a "calling." While that term can feel heavy in today's world, I believe it is quite simple. Coaching is about passing on the love and support we once received as players. It is about being a consistent, steady presence for young men who may be searching for guidance, just as we once did. Coaching is not about strategies, wins, or losses. It is about creating a space where players feel valued, supported, and loved both on and off the field. That is the true reward of coaching, and it is what makes it so fulfilling.

With that in mind, take a minute to think about the following questions in regards to your role as a coach:

- How does your role as a coach impact your responsibilities as a father, husband, or mentor in your own family?

- What do your players truly need from you, beyond just coaching?

- How much support do your players receive at home, whether with schoolwork or emotional encouragement?

- Who is their biggest cheerleader at home—or do they even have one?

- Do you know what they go home to each night?

- Were they read to as children? Do they eat dinner alone? Will they even eat dinner tonight?

- And most importantly, what would their lives look like without sports?

As coaches, we are responsible for far more than developing game plans or teaching skills. As competitive individuals, we sometimes focus too much on tactics and strategies, forgetting what truly matters. We have the opportunity and the responsibility to deeply influence the lives of young people. It is important to find moments during or after practice to have conversations with your players that shed light on these types of questions. It is also crucial that those outside the coaching profession understand the depth of this role and the impact we can have.

Growing up without a father figure during my adolescence, I never truly grasped what I had missed until I became a parent myself. The first time I held my sons, and as I watched their love for their mother grow, I realized just how much was absent in my own childhood. The profound and tragic effects of fatherlessness became painfully clear when contrasted with the love I experienced the first time I ever held my boys. Hold your baby for the first time, and you will understand exactly what I mean.

For me, sports and the guidance of my coaches provided solace. By applying their lessons, I earned their respect and attention. They gave me stability and purpose during a time when I needed it most. I often wonder where I might have ended up without high school football. Coaching was not a family tradition for me, but football ignited something within me. It was a spark that led to countless opportunities and realizations I might never have discovered otherwise.

Coaching is about far more than the X's and O's. It is about love, guidance, and creating a foundation where young people can thrive, even when life off the field feels uncertain or unstable. It is a privilege to be part of that journey, and it is why coaching continues to be such a meaningful part of my life.

While there is no definitive statistic about how many high school football coaches grew up without fathers, talk to enough of them and a pattern emerges. Many experienced the absence of a consistent male role model in their own lives, a wound that quietly fueled their purpose. For these coaches, the field became more than a place to teach plays; it became a way to offer what they once needed most. A steady, trustworthy presence for the next generation.

Sports provide more than competition; they create connection and offer a chance to be seen and understood in ways that are often unavailable elsewhere. I owe much of who I am today to the coaches who shaped my life. Coaching gave me the tools to grow not only as a man but also as a Christian, a father, and a husband, imperfect yet striving. That profound impact is what inspired me to write this book: to remind both new and veteran coaches of what truly matters and why we do what we do. If we fail to build on the lessons we were taught or lose sight of where we came from, our efforts risk becoming meaningless. The values we hold dear can be lost if we do not intentionally fight to preserve them. And if we allow the cold and timid souls, those who criticize from the sidelines but never step into the arena, to dictate the narrative, the difference we make as coaches will eventually fade.

At its core, the most valuable gift a coach can give is presence. High school coaches are more than play-callers or strategists; they are role models, often without their players even realizing it. Through mentorship, young men are guided into adulthood by coaches who step into the gaps left in their lives. This role far outweighs mastering an air raid offense or designing the perfect game plan, which many mistakenly assume is a coach's primary responsibility.

I am not a psychologist, and this book does not claim to solve the issue of fatherlessness. But I want to leave you with this: walk into any high school locker room or weight room in America, and you will feel it. The tension. The unspoken questions. The hunger, not just for a scholarship or a starting position, but for something deeper. For direction. For belonging. For a man to look them in the eye and say, "You matter."

We live in a time when millions of boys are growing up without a consistent male role model at home. Fatherlessness is not just a social issue; it is a soul issue. It leaves a void, and whether they realize it or not, many players step onto the field each day carrying that emptiness. They will not say it out loud. They may even try to hide it. But they are watching. They are listening. They are learning how to be men, not from your words, but from how you show up every single day.

You might be the most consistent man in a player's life. Do not underestimate the weight of that responsibility. Coaching today is about far more than drawing up plays or breaking down film. You are not just teaching football. You are standing in the gap. You shape how young men face failure, respond to criticism, treat others, and endure adversity. Often, you are the only man teaching these lessons to young men who are struggling or even lost.

Some of these boys are familiar with instability, broken promises, and silence at the dinner table. They are used to being yelled at or ignored. But when you correct them with respect, when you show up early, when you pull them aside and say, "I'm proud of you," you offer something many of them have never experienced from a man. No, you are not their father, and you do not need to replace one. But your presence, your standards, and your belief in them become anchors. They learn what manhood looks like, not from a speech, but from your example.

When I was a kid, I learned to tie a fishing knot from the back of a hook package simply because I had no one to teach me and I wanted to fish. In the years since I became a father, there have been times when I have taken my boys fishing, and their poles got what I call "unexplainably tangled." While I might initially have thrown a fit in frustration, in the middle of doing so I always remembered spending most of my youth fishing alone. That memory still comes as a jolt and serves as a reminder that I am capable of doing better for my boys.

Up front, I am far from a perfect dad, and I often re-live situations with my boys where I could have been more patient, more helpful, or even tougher. Honestly, even when I come up short, however, I almost always justify my actions with the thought, "Nobody did this for me; I must do it for them." Maybe this sounds selfish or even egotistical, but this is one of those times when it is important to me to be vulnerable and open in sharing these very human feelings as a father navigating uncharted territory. If you are a father, if you are a real coach, you, too, know what it is like to who sometimes feels like a barbarian, ill-equipped to give his kids all the love they need from their father. You know what it is like to wonder what else you might have done, what you might have done differently, what you could have said or not said.

If we are honest, each of us often wonder if we are doing a good job as a father, as a coach-father. Of this, however, I am sure. I hope that one day my sons will look back and remember a joyful childhood with a good dad who loved them and of fond memories of time spent with me.

I know I am not a bad dad, but I'd be lying if I said being a good one was easy. At times, I feel like I am doing a pretty good job. Then there are times when I feel like I'm failing, like I am not doing enough. Maybe I seem unhappy while dragging the canoe two miles, or grumpy while cleaning deer with the boys, or ready to strangle one of them in the backseat on a long drive. I'm not sure if I am harder on myself as a dad because I never experienced this kind of fatherhood myself, or if this is just how it's supposed to be. All I know is that I am doing my best, and I love my boys so much.

Growing up, I do not recall ever being hugged by the man I called dad, and as a father, I am determined to give them what I did not have, what I so desperately needed even though I might not have been able to put it into words. Maybe because of what I did not have, every time I hug my boys, it feels like I am giving myself a hug. Regardless of what else is going on in life, nothing is more incredible than the feeling I have when holding my boys. I like to think that in those moments, I am passing on strength and love they might not fully understand until they become fathers themselves, that I am giving them love, courage, faith, grace, and everything that defines being a father who truly loves his kids. If my boys become even better fathers than me because of what I have tried to give, I will be absolutely over the moon proud! Becoming a grandfather will be a second-generation fatherhood, watching my boys father their children, while I get to be the ultimate grandpa - always ready with s'mores, juice boxes, and an excuse to get outside and get dirty!

Kobe Bryant once said, "Leadership is lonely.... If you're going to be a leader, you're not going to please everybody. You've got to hold people accountable." Bryant nailed it. As a coach, as a father, true leadership, true parenting, is not about being liked by everyone; it is about having the courage to enforce values and protect what matters most.

Unfortunately, we live in a time when many teams and organizations have abandoned their standards, and it shows. That is why platforms like Armageddon Coach exist: to remind us of the courage it takes to lead, to protect what we hold dear, to influence others in a positive way and to" leave it on the field." If we as an Armageddon Coach do these things, we will end our days knowing that because we have given our all, we will stand tall, having no regrets, never questioning if we could have done more - even if we stand alone in the arena.

Leadership is not easy, but it is essential. Here's my challenge to you: keep showing up. Keep speaking the truth. Keep standing firm. In a world filled with chaos and uncertainty, you may be the one steady voice a young person remembers for the rest of their life. Teach them the difference between right and wrong.

And to any players reading this who don't have a father figure in their life by that person's choice, know this: it is not okay that they chose to walk away. That burden is on them, not you. While you cannot control their decisions, you can control your response. It is your responsibility to rise above the hand you have been dealt. Be stronger. Be better. Prove that where you come from does not define where you are going.

Coaches, you signed up to teach football, but what you are doing is so much more.

You are shaping futures.
You are breaking cycles.
You are changing lives, often in ways you may never fully see.

COACH'S REFLECTION

As a coach, you have the incredible opportunity to shape not only the athletic abilities of young athletes but also their character and values. Your influence extends beyond the field, touching families and encouraging growth in meaningful ways. Take a moment to reflect on your role and how it aligns with fostering godly leadership and building positive relationships within families.

Here are some key questions to guide your reflection:

- How do my coaching methods demonstrate integrity, faith, and compassion?

- Am I intentional about prioritizing character development alongside athletic performance?

- How can I inspire fathers or guardians to actively support their child's personal and spiritual growth?

- Do I create an environment where lessons from the field translate into life skills beyond sports?

- What steps can I take to ensure my role strengthens relationships between fathers and their children?

Use these reflections as a guide to evaluate your impact and to challenge yourself to make a lasting difference in the lives of the athletes and families you serve. The influence you carry reaches far beyond the game. Let it inspire growth, connection, and transformation both on and off the field.

CHAPTER 10
COACHING GENERATION Z LEARNERS

I am fortunate to come from one of the most respected coaching trees in Texas high school football, guided by Godly men who are not only some of the best teachers in the world but also incredible role models. I firmly believe that every kid can learn, no matter their learning styles, differences, or shortcomings. I have witnessed this truth firsthand countless times. Being a coach is a role I hold with immense pride, and I deeply respect the impact this profession has on the lives of young people.

A great coach has the power to transform a 160-pound player into someone who feels and plays like a 260-pound gladiator on the field. That transformation begins with instilling confidence and providing guidance, equipping athletes with a clear understanding of how to execute their assignments with precision, play after play, often up to 70 times per game. Smart players play fast, and at the end of the day, the teams winning state championships are often the ones whose players have learned and grown more throughout the season than their opponents. Success is not just about peaking physically at the right time; it is about peaking mentally as well.

Today's generation of learners, often referred to as the "anxious generation," presents new challenges for coaches. These young people face unprecedented pressures and distractions, which makes our role as coaches more crucial than ever. We must do more than teach plays; we must guide, inspire, and create environments where players can face their fears and rise to their potential. Real coaches understand this. Above all else, they are exceptional teachers.

I am a coach to my core, and my passion lies in helping young people learn, grow, and thrive both on and off the field. If you do not share that same passion, perhaps it is time to reflect, because real coaches are not just about the X's and O's. They are about building people.

High school football is a crucible where young athletes are molded, tested, and prepared for the complexities of life. Today, the landscape is evolving as Generation Z steps onto the field, bringing unique characteristics and learning styles that challenge traditional coaching methods. Understanding both these changes and the constants is essential for coaches who want to maximize their players' potential in an era defined by rapid information exchange and constant distraction.

With the rise of technology and social media, Generation Z has grown up in a digital world that is always shifting. They are accustomed to instant gratification and often have shorter attention spans than previous generations. As a result, coaches must adapt their approach to effectively communicate with and engage this new generation of athletes. One significant change brought by Generation Z is the rise of player empowerment. With access to information at their fingertips, young athletes are more aware of their value and potential than ever before. This can lead to challenges including dealing with egos and managing expectations, but it also presents an opportunity for coaches to empower their players by involving them in decision-making processes and, even better, the learning process.

CHARACTERISTICS OF GENERATION Z ATHLETES

Generation Z, born roughly between 1997 and 2012, is the first cohort to grow up with the internet and digital technology at their fingertips. This connectivity shapes their worldview and learning preferences.

They are adept at multitasking, absorbing information quickly, and are visual learners, often engaging more effectively with digital content than with traditional textbooks. This digital immersion however, also means they are susceptible to information overload, which can hinder concentration and focus on the field and in the classroom.

Furthermore, Generation Z values authenticity and transparency, seeking genuine connections with coaches and teammates. They also have a strong sense of social responsibility and are more likely to be socially conscious and advocate for causes in which they believe. As coaches, it is essential to understand these characteristics and use them to develop a positive team culture that fosters trust, open communication, and a sense of purpose.

ADAPTING COACHING METHODS

To effectively coach today's generation of athletes, it is essential to adapt traditional methods to fit their learning styles and preferences. This includes incorporating technology into training sessions, using visual aids such as videos or graphics in game plans, and providing instant feedback through digital platforms like WARDBORD. Additionally, coaches should also create flexible and dynamic training environments that allow for frequent breaks, as Generation Z athletes often benefit more from shorter bursts of focused activity than from long, sustained practices.

Equally important is the way coaches communicate with their players. Patience and intentionality are vital. Today's athletes are growing up in a time when strong communication and listening skills are not always emphasized. While they will adapt, it is crucial for coaches to over-communicate and be deliberate in teaching what truly matters. This is especially important when working with younger athletes, starting with middle schoolers. By setting clear expectations and reinforcing key concepts consistently, we can help players develop the skills they need to succeed both on and off the field.

Furthermore, coaches must consider the impact of social media on their players. With the potential to reach a large audience instantly, social media can be both a powerful tool and a dangerous distraction. Because of this, it is essential for coaches to educate athletes about responsible social media use and establish guidelines for appropriate online behavior to protect their privacy, reputation, and team dynamics. By fostering strong communication and building trust, coaches can better guide players through the unique challenges of today's digital age.

Perhaps the most critical point is helping players become more comfortable with communication and self-expression, which is often a weak area for this generation. It is unrealistic to expect young athletes to naturally excel at clear and confident communication, especially in a world dominated by screens and instant messaging. Instead, coaches must meet players where they are, acknowledging these challenges without labeling them as faults. Over-communicating and teaching foundational skills such as listening attentively, making eye contact, and articulating thoughts clearly are vital steps in their development. While it is fair to challenge players to grow and work hard in this area, coaches must first emphasize the importance of communication and provide practical support to help them improve.

Generation Z athletes are presented with unique challenges shaped by how they communicate and process information. Raised as digital natives, they are more comfortable texting or instant messaging than engaging in face-to-face conversations. Many struggle with nonverbal cues, eye contact, and sustained dialogue. Research even suggests that their vocabulary and communication skills, including reading ability, are weaker compared to previous generations.

Attention spans are another major hurdle, shortened by constant digital stimulation. Coaches often find themselves condensing meetings into just three key points to maintain focus, since long lectures or extended team discussions risk losing players entirely. To be effective, coaching today's athletes requires adaptability, clarity, and a commitment to developing strong communication skills both on and off the field.

Feedback presents its own challenge. Gen Z athletes thrive on frequent input, yet they often take criticism very personally, internalizing even mild remarks in ways that can undermine their confidence. This heightened sensitivity demands a more intentional approach from coaches, one that balances honesty with encouragement to keep athletes both engaged and motivated.

At the root of this dynamic, is a broader cultural shift in attitudes toward authority. Gen Z players are far less likely to accept the traditional "because I said so" approach. Instead, they seek clarity, collaboration, and purpose. Research shows that this generation wants to understand the "why" behind instructions and responds best when coaches involve them in the process while communicating with clear intention.

For coaches, these realities demand adaptation. Communication must be clear, concise, and frequent. Feedback should be constructive and respectful, as well. Above all, athletes need to feel heard. Without this intentional effort, these communication gaps can quickly become roadblocks to learning and team cohesion.

This brings me to a critical point: coaches who neglect their middle school programs are setting themselves up for long-term failure. Developing athletes at this stage is more important than ever. And this does not mean simply placing the "right" coach in charge at the middle school level. It means every coach, regardless of experience or position, should be willing and eager to invest in younger players. No coach should view themselves as too advanced or too impatient for middle school athletes. In fact, a reluctance to work with them often signals a deeper issue, such as a lack of motivation or effort. Not always, but it is worth considering.

Coaching middle school athletes requires maturity, patience, effective communication, and a deliberate approach to teaching. This age group forms the foundation not only for future athletic success but also for the development of life skills and personal growth. The true difference between exceptional programs and average ones often lies in how well they nurture players at this level.

The days of coaches begrudgingly attending middle school

practices, standing idly with other coaches, and yelling at players out of frustration or poor communication are over. That approach was never effective, and today it is downright harmful. Middle school is the stage where potential athletes begin to grasp discipline, effort, and the fundamentals of the game. Coaches have a responsibility to guide them, not only in their sport but also in life.

At this level, coaches must be fully engaged. Learn the players' names. Help them put on their equipment if they're struggling. Over-communicate when teaching drills. Never put them down, even jokingly. Avoid yelling at a player before you've taken the time to understand them. Your role is to help them find their voice, build their confidence, and learn how to communicate effectively. If your players merely *like* you, it is a sign you are not doing enough. But if they *love* you, it means you are leading the right way.

Investing in middle school athletes is no longer optional. It is the foundation of future success. Let's give these young players the guidance, support, and respect they deserve.

THE EVOLVING ROLE OF COACHES

Today's coaches are more than tactical experts; they are mentors, motivators, and digital navigators. To reach their athletes, they must adapt to diverse learning styles while embracing technology and innovative strategies. This means using tools such as video analysis, digital playbooks, and interactive learning platforms that align with Generation Z's digital-native mindset. Equally important, coaches must remain sensitive to the mental and emotional development and well-being of their players. In a world shaped by social media and societal pressures, coaches often serve as a steady, grounding influence.

Navigating the gridiron with Generation Z requires a thorough understanding of their unique characteristics and learning preferences. By adapting coaching methods and embracing technology, coaches can maximize their players' potential and foster a positive team culture that empowers and motivates this generation of athletes. As the landscape continues to evolve, coaches must remain adaptable and open-minded, continuously seeking new ways to engage, connect, and develop their players both on and off the field.

COMPETITIVE LEARNING ADVANTAGE

To give players a competitive edge, it is important for coaches to focus on holistic development. This includes fostering not just physical skills but also cognitive flexibility, emotional resilience, strategic thinking and the physiological needs of players and coaches. Techniques such as visualization, mindfulness, and situational simulations are incorporated into training regimens to enhance mental acuity and decision-making under pressure. Coaches are tasked with creating an environment where learning from mistakes is as valued as achieving success, promoting a growth mindset that prepares players for both sports and life challenges.

Moreover, the evaluation of performance introduces friction in the minds of players, which ultimately generates learning. This is emphasized through eight critical evaluation points.

- **Accountability**: Position coaches play a vital role in setting clear expectations and delivering consistent feedback. Every play counts, and it is essential to review them thoroughly so players understand whether they executed their assignments correctly and gave maximum effort. Constructive feedback should never be avoided. Even if a player makes mistakes on 15 out of 60 plays, that means they were successful on 45 plays and represents an overall 75 percent success rate.

- **Defining Performance**: Today's athletes crave feedback and value being held to a high standard.

When coaches provide honest assessments and challenge players to grow, they not only improve performance on the field but also prepare young athletes for the greater demands of life beyond football.

- **Defining Performance**: Performance is the successful execution of an assignment. In football, this means every player fulfills their role on each play. With 11 assignments per snap, success depends on total team execution. Offensively, every play is designed to score a touchdown in a perfect scenario where each defensive player is accounted for. However, it only takes one missed assignment to derail the effort. Consistent execution is the foundation of team success.

- **Comparing Performance**: Use game performance to evaluate players on a weekly basis and identify specific areas for growth. Players may not always see how their individual execution connects to the final score. By breaking down assignments and setting clear, measurable goals, such as improving execution by 20 assignments compared to the previous week, you provide them with tangible progress to pursue. Winning by a wide margin is rewarding, but true development comes from consistently raising the level of execution, not simply relying on the scoreboard.

- **Differentiating Performance Week to Week**: Analyze performance across wins and losses using analytics. For example, showing players that they executed fewer assignments in a high-scoring win than in a close victory reveals that the scoreboard does not always reflect true performance. Consistency in execution is the key to sustained success, making it the most important coaching metric.

- **Emphasizing the Bigger Picture**: Keep players grounded in team goals by demonstrating the cumulative impact of missed assignments throughout a season. Metrics such as execution and effort should be tied to long-term objectives, reinforcing how these elements contribute to postseason success. Teach them to be student-athletes who prioritize effort and execution on every play. Peaking at the right time during the season comes from consistently focusing on what truly drives success.

- **Prioritizing Great Effort as Measurable**: Effort and execution, once viewed as intangible qualities, can and should be measured. Effort must be evaluated on every play, regardless of whether a player is directly involved in the action. Missed opportunities to give maximum effort can cost a team in pivotal moments. To make effort measurable, coaches must first define what great effort looks like and communicate those standards clearly to both players and staff. Just as importantly, they must define what poor effort looks like. Holding athletes accountable to this standard not only strengthens team culture but also equips players with the resilience and discipline they need for success in football and in life.

- **Developing Players' Football IQ**: Elevating a team's football IQ is essential to sustained success. Programs that emphasize intelligence at every position consistently outperform their competition. Winning teams are not built solely on standout athletes, but also through the development of their average players to achieve a deeper understanding of the game. By investing in learning, coaches create a competitive edge and foster teams capable of thriving at the highest level. Talent alone cannot secure championships; it must be paired with strategy, disciplined execution, and a comprehensive understanding of the game.

EVOLVING TEACHING METHODS AND PLAYER RETENTION

Coaching has always been grounded in timeless values such as discipline, respect, and perseverance. While these principles remain constant, the methods of teaching and player development have evolved. What was once driven largely by repetition and rote learning has now shifted toward adaptive, personalized approaches, much like individualized education plans in academics. Coaches today understand that athletes process and retain information in different ways, and embracing these differences is essential for fostering real growth.

HOW BLOOM'S TAXONOMY ENHANCES COACHING

One framework that has reshaped modern coaching is Bloom's Taxonomy. Originally designed for educational settings, it provides a structured approach to cognitive development. When applied to sports, Bloom's Taxonomy allows coaches to create training plans that deepen players' understanding, enhance performance, and foster long-term success.

This doesn't mean discarding traditional coaching methods.

Instead, it involves blending proven practices with innovative strategies to meet the needs of today's athletes. By applying Bloom's Taxonomy to sports, we can provide coaches with a learning-focused framework that helps them become more intentional in their teaching. The best coaches are expert teachers who find ways for every athlete to learn.

In business, there's a saying: "What gets measured gets improved." This principle applies directly to coaching—if we measure player learning, it will also improve. That's why having a structured framework is essential for intentionally developing our players' skills and understanding. Let's explore how these concepts apply to coaching.

TAILORING TRAINING TO INDIVIDUAL NEEDS

Athletes learn differently, and Bloom's Taxonomy helps coaches identify where each player is in their cognitive development. Starting with foundational skills like "remembering" and "understanding," athletes can progress toward advanced skills like "analyzing" and "creating." For example, a coach might initially focus on memorizing defensive formations before advancing to breaking down opponents' strategies and innovating new plays.

SETTING CLEAR LEARNING OBJECTIVES

Bloom's Taxonomy uses actionable verbs like "interpret," "analyze," and "create" to help coaches set specific goals. In coaching, similar terms like "read," "decide," and "trigger" can be integrated into daily drills to help execute game plans. For example, a coach could set an objective: "Analyze game footage to identify how to stop the power read." Clear objectives ensure athletes understand what is expected of them and how to succeed. Simplifying the goal helps players practice and play with a clear mind, knowing exactly what the team needs them to do.

BALANCING PHYSICAL SKILLS WITH CRITICAL THINKING

Training sessions can combine physical drills ("applying" skills) with mental exercises ("evaluating" team performance or "understanding" game strategies). This balance builds technical ability and sharpens mental agility, preparing athletes to excel in high-pressure situations. However, many position coaches avoid dedicated teaching time on the field, fearing how it might look to a head coach. I always respected my offensive line coach for meticulously walking us through our plays, adapted for each week's specific defense. It's not just okay to slow down and teach your players on the field—it is essential for their development.

ENCOURAGING CREATIVITY AND INNOVATION

Higher-order thinking, like "analyzing" plays or "creating" new tactics, leads to more engaging and interactive coaching. Encouraging athletes to innovate fosters confidence and adaptability—key traits for success in competitive sports. While I always prepare a specific plan for each opponent, I remain open to feedback from players. It's okay to ask your players for their opinion; you might be surprised by a great idea. When that happens, act on their input and incorporate it. Your players will play harder for you when they've contributed to the strategy.

USING ASSESSMENTS TO TRACK PROGRESS

Bloom's Taxonomy helps coaches design structured assessments to track an athlete's progress. For instance, athletes can be evaluated on their ability to recall plays, apply techniques, and assess their own performance. These assessments provide valuable feedback and inform future coaching strategies. Over time, this approach not only improves skills but also develops smarter, more self-aware athletes equipped to handle the mental and physical demands of the game. While tools like WARDBORD are effective for tracking in-game performance, assessing off-season instruction is equally crucial. Measuring this progress provides feedback that drives continuous learning and improvement.

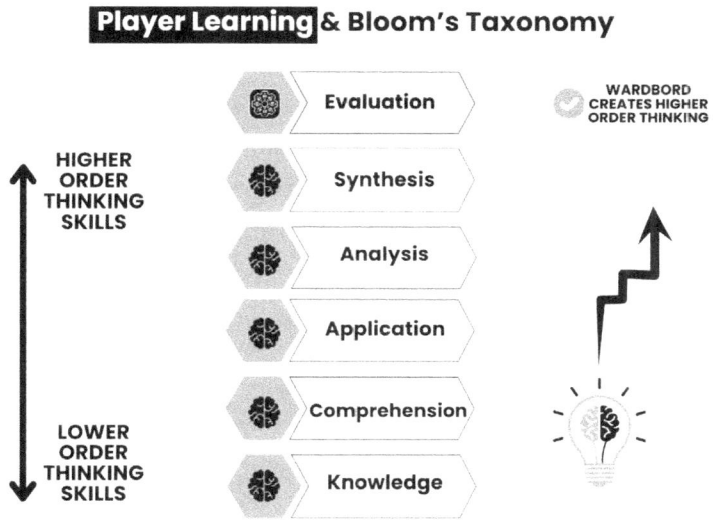

THE ROLE OF INNOVATION IN COACHING

The best coaches are those who honor traditional methods while embracing innovation and adaptability. They recognize that players learn differently and adjust their teaching accordingly. This shift does not mean players are "soft" or "lazy." Instead, it reflects the evolution of learning styles and the necessity of modern approaches. By blending proven coaching principles with frameworks such as Bloom's Taxonomy, coaches create an environment where athletes can thrive both physically and mentally.

Coaching extends beyond teaching skills; it is about fostering growth on and off the field. When coaches understand how athletes learn and leverage tools like Bloom's Taxonomy, they set the stage for success that reaches beyond the scoreboard. The result is a team of players equipped not only to outplay their opponents but also to outthink and outperform them in every facet of competition.

A critical component of modern coaching is understanding how players learn and retain information. This is where Hermann Ebbinghaus's research on the "forgetting curve" becomes especially important. Ebbinghaus demonstrated that without reinforcement or repetition, retention drops sharply, often within just 24 hours. For coaches, this finding highlights the importance of structured repetition, practical application, and varied methods of reinforcement. By reviewing concepts frequently and applying them in different contexts, coaches help athletes retain strategies and skills more effectively, strengthening both performance and long-term development.

Instead of delivering all instruction at once during team or position meetings, innovative coaches break plays and techniques into smaller, more manageable segments. These concepts are revisited consistently over time, which helps ensure they stick. Video analysis reinforces these lessons, while encouraging players to reflect on their performance shortly after a game leverages what Hermann Ebbinghaus called the "spacing effect," the principle that spreading learning over multiple sessions improves long-term retention. The goal is straightforward: help players remember what they learn. While this may sound obvious, applying research on how the brain works can dramatically improve how athletes absorb and retain information.

It is easy to blame modern distractions for why players forget, but the reality is more nuanced. Players today are not forgetting more than they used to; they are forgetting at the same rate, depending on how information is presented and how often it is reinforced. What has changed is the sheer volume of content competing for their attention. Because players are inundated with information, the risk of missing essential football concepts increases unless coaches adapt their teaching methods to meet the needs of modern learners.

Research shows that retention rates can increase by 50 percent or more when strategies such as spaced repetition, active recall, and multi-sensory learning are applied. Coaches who integrate these methods help players not only remember plays and strategies but also build confidence and develop muscle memory. This approach strengthens both the mental and physical dimensions of performance, producing athletes who are skilled, adaptable, and prepared to excel under pressure.

Importantly, these adjustments do not require coaches to abandon what already works. Instead, they involve rethinking the sequence and frequency of practices, both on and off the field. By refining how lessons are delivered and reinforced, coaches can significantly improve how players absorb and retain critical knowledge, equipping them to succeed in today's demanding environment.

By blending timeless values such as discipline and respect with modern insights into how memory and learning function, forward-thinking coaches are reshaping player development. Beyond teaching the game, they adopt strategies to counter the forgetting curve, ensuring players retain essential knowledge while remaining engaged and supported.

The following concepts outline how coaches can improve retention and empower the next generation of athletes:

- **Leverage the Spacing Effect**: Provide focused feedback over time through regular learning campaigns. Spacing out learning boosts retention and deepens understanding.

- **Use Clear Metrics with Coaches' Notes**: Offer players detailed notes with clear metrics and actionable insights, connecting feedback to tangible improvements.

- **Ensure Digital Access to Learning**: Digitize learning materials so players can review feedback and resources anytime, enhancing their ability to revisit and retain lessons.

- **Prioritize Sleep and Recovery**: Encourage players to focus on sleep by optimizing schedules. Adequate rest (8–10 hours) is essential for memory retention and physical recovery.

- **Promote Mixing of Topics**: Mix up learning topics instead of focusing on one area at a time. This reduces interference and strengthens long-term memory.

- **Build a Culture of Learning**: Foster a team-wide commitment to continuous growth, integrating these strategies to support both individual and collective development.

The best coaches are lifelong learners themselves, because they must constantly refine their methods to inspire and empower their players for lasting success.

EXPLORING EFFECTIVE LEARNING STRATEGIES FOR TODAY'S YOUTH

The brain development of today's youth is deeply influenced by their digital environment. Neuroscience shows that constant interaction with technology shapes attention spans and processing speeds. While this can be an advantage in high-pressure situations such as making quick decisions during competition, it also highlights the need for strategies that strengthen focus, build resilience, and reduce anxiety. Coaches who recognize these cognitive and emotional factors can design training programs that align with how modern youth learn and perform.

One effective framework for structuring learning is the Player Learning Pyramid, which is grounded in research on retention rates across different teaching methods. The base of the pyramid emphasizes approaches with the highest retention rates, while the top reflects methods with the lowest. Studies consistently show that athletes retain up to 90 percent of what they learn when they teach others or engage in active practice, while passive methods such as lectures or reading result in only 5 to 10 percent retention. By applying this model, coaches can create environments that maximize both learning and retention, ensuring players develop not just skills but lasting understanding.

PLAYER LEARNING PYRAMID RETENTION RATES

- **5%**: Retention from lectures or passive listening. (e.g., team and position meetings).

- **10%**: Retention from reading material. (e.g.,scouting reports).

- **20%**: Retention from audiovisual materials (e.g., video analysis).

- **30%**: Retention from demonstrations or observing others.

- **50%**: Retention from group discussions or interactive dialogue.

- **75%**: Retention from practice by doing (e.g., drills, scrimmages).

- **90%**: Retention from teaching others or immediate application.

TEACHING STRATEGIES TO IMPROVE PLAYER RETENTION

Retention is crucial for player development, and understanding how athletes learn is the foundation for long-term success. Research, including the Learning Pyramid, emphasizes that hands-on, interactive methods are the most effective for retention. By integrating these principles, coaches can create smarter, more prepared teams. Here are key strategies to enhance player learning and retention:

1. TEAM MEETINGS AND DISCUSSIONS

Team meetings give players the chance to discuss strategies, break down plays, and actively participate in meaningful conversations. When these discussions are supported with detailed notes from coaches, players walk away with actionable insights and a stronger understanding of what is expected of them. This active involvement not only improves communication but also enhances retention. Studies show that players remember close to 50 percent of the information when they engage in discussions, compared to much lower retention when the learning is limited to passive methods such as listening or reading.

2. VIDEO REVIEW SESSIONS

Video analysis is an essential tool for connecting feedback to performance. Reviewing game or practice footage helps players visually identify areas of improvement and success, enhancing their ability to apply feedback to real-game scenarios. Combining visual learning with active observation improves retention and reinforces key lessons.

3. POSITION-SPECIFIC MEETINGS

Small group or position-focused meetings provide targeted coaching tailored to specific roles on the field. Narrowing the focus allows players to absorb more information relevant to their responsibilities, making the learning process more effective and applicable.

4. WALK-THROUGHS AND PRACTICE REPS

Hands-on practice is one of the most effective ways to improve retention, with physical engagement topping the Learning Pyramid at 75%. Walk-throughs and practice reps allow players to actively apply feedback in real-time, solidifying skills and preparing them for competition.

5. INTERACTIVE FEEDBACK SESSIONS

Dynamic, interactive feedback is a powerful tool that helps players retain up to 90% of what they learn. Personalized, engaging feedback allows players to revisit insights, explore areas for growth, and continuously improve their performance.

6. REST AND RECOVERY FOR BETTER LEARNING

Rest plays a critical role in memory retention. Research shows that 8 - 10 hours of sleep helps consolidate learning, ensuring players better retain information from practices and meetings. Coaches can support this by optimizing schedules and reducing unnecessary commitments, prioritizing recovery time.

7. BUILDING A CULTURE OF LEARNING AND GROWTH

Fostering a learning-focused environment is essential for long-term team success. By incorporating active learning techniques, structured feedback, and a commitment to growth, coaches can empower players to continuously improve and perform at their highest level.

Moving beyond passive teaching methods, these strategies create an engaging, hands-on environment that strengthens retention and builds a foundation for both individual and team development. Incorporating models like the Player Learning Pyramid and other research-backed approaches enhances skill acquisition while also supporting greater player retention and overall well-being. Technology tools such as WARDBORD, which provide interactive feedback, further reinforce these methods. By combining traditional coaching values with innovative learning strategies, coaches can equip athletes to excel not only physically but also cognitively and emotionally in their sport.

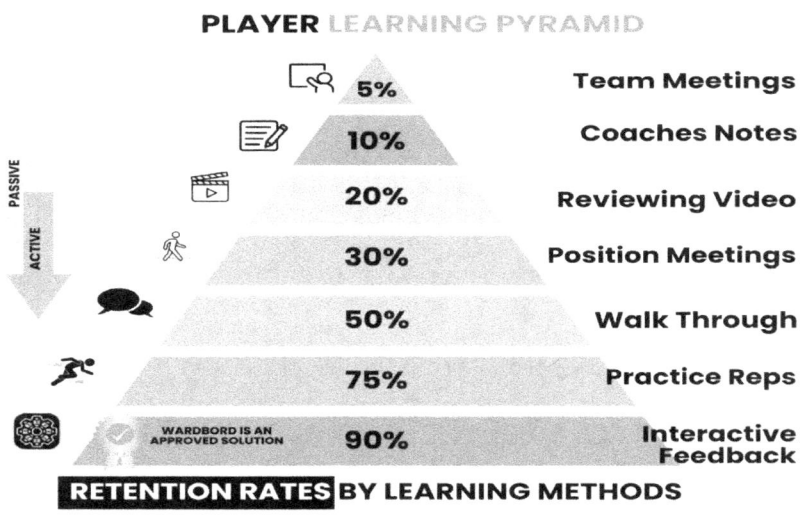

The key takeaway is simple: if you can teach, you can coach. If you cannot teach, you will never be an effective coach, no matter how much you know about football or any other sport. Knowledge without the ability to communicate and instill it in others has little impact.

Too often, I have seen coaches resort to berating players, shouting instructions, and clinging to a "hard-nosed" approach, convinced that yelling is the only way to motivate. The truth is, players rarely absorb anything in those moments. Being loud is not the same as being heard.

The best coaches recognize that teaching is the foundation of coaching. They value individual drills and practice time, but they also know when to pause the action. Sometimes it means stopping a drill, gathering the group, and walking through a concept. It means asking questions, listening for understanding, and making sure players truly grasp what is being taught. Other times, it means breaking the routine, lightening the mood with a joke, or inviting a quieter player to share one of their own. Relationships must come first, because without trust and connection, meaningful learning cannot take place.

Coaches should also embrace experimentation and lean into moments of friction during practice or throughout the season. Progress often stalls during predictable stretches such as fall camp, spring practices, or those long weeks when players grow tired of competing against one another and long for that first scrimmage against new opponents. These are not setbacks; they are opportunities.

In these pivotal moments, great coaches step outside the ordinary. They find creative ways to spark growth, reframe challenges, and push players to see the game and themselves differently. By approaching these situations with intention, creativity, and patience, you not only keep players engaged but also ensure they are constantly learning, evolving, and thriving under your leadership.

COACH'S REFLECTION

Reflecting on your role as a coach is essential for growth and maximizing your impact on your athletes. Use these prompts to evaluate how you inspire, guide, and connect with your team:

- In what ways are you fostering trust and respect with your athletes? Are there opportunities to strengthen these relationships?

- How do your actions and habits demonstrate leadership, both during practices and in your daily life?

- Can you recall a time when your guidance positively impacted an athlete's life beyond sports? How did that experience shape you as a coach?

- How do you balance offering praise with constructive feedback? Are there ways to enhance your communication style?

- What core values do you aim to instill in your athletes, and how do your coaching practices align with those values?

- Reflect on the lessons you've learned from your athletes—how have they influenced your coaching methods and perspective?

- What kind of legacy do you want to leave as a coach, and what steps can you take now to bring that vision to life?

Taking time to reflect on these questions can help you refine your approach, deepen your impact, and continue to grow as a mentor and leader.

CHAPTER 11

THE LOST BOYS OF DADDY BALL

THE ROLE OF COACHES IN SHAPING GENERATION Z ATHLETES: BALANCING MENTAL HEALTH AND LIFELONG IMPACT

High school sports carry undeniable allure, as H. G. Bissinger captured in *Friday Night Lights*. He revealed both the magnetic pull of youth athletics and the dangers of adults living vicariously through their children, warning how quickly a young athlete's passion can fade. Hall of Fame baseball player Alex Rodriguez once noted that 95 percent of young athletes feel like quitting their sport, often during the car ride home after a game. This striking statistic underscores the fragile mental and emotional state many athletes face today and the critical role that parents and coaches play in shaping their experiences.

As a coach, I have come to see the deep connection between mental health, emotional well-being, and the relationships we build with our players. These factors directly influence how athletes learn and grow - not only as players, but as people. It is essential for parents and coaches to recognize the profound impact we have during these formative years. The "blank slates" coaches worked with decades ago no longer exist.

Today's athletes often arrive carrying emotional weight shaped by the complexities of modern life. Our responsibility is to adapt, to meet them where they are, and to guide them forward. The cards we are dealt may look different, but we can still play them with purpose and make a lasting difference.

ADDRESSING MENTAL AND EMOTIONAL HEALTH IN YOUTH SPORTS

Dr. Peter Gray, a renowned psychologist, has extensively studied how the reduction of children's freedom in modern society negatively impacts their development. He argues that, historically, children have always been free to play and explore, except during periods of intense child labor or slavery. Gray links this loss of freedom, especially in play and exploration, to rising anxiety, depression, and helplessness in children and teens. He asserts that "Children learn the most important lessons in life through self-directed play, where they confront challenges, take risks, and develop their own solutions."

Gray emphasizes that structured schedules and a focus on academic achievement have crowded out opportunities for unstructured play, which is essential for growth. When I first came across Dr. Gray's research, I couldn't help but compare his references to "structured schedules" and "academic achievement" to how many parents today push their children toward select baseball and other club sports. I think about the kids playing 4th-grade football who practice three times a week and have a game on the weekend, all while playing rec basketball and taking hitting lessons to get ready for baseball in the spring. It seems we live in a world where it is easy to forget that sometimes less is more. We run our children ragged, believing we're molding them into elite athletes. Or, if not that, we're obsessively ensuring they're labeled gifted in school, taking all the "right" classes to graduate at the top. We deny them opportunities to fail and the space to breathe outside our predetermined expectations. Often, we don't even ask children what they need, assuming we already know, based on societal norms and influences. Gray's research links the decline in free play with an erosion of children's intrinsic motivation and creativity. Citing data, he notes that over the last 50 years, time spent on free play has drastically decreased while time allocated to schooling and homework has climbed significantly. "We are depriving children of their natural means of learning about the world and coping with it," says Gray.

Supporting his claims, Gray's work is bolstered by studies indicating that play is critical to the development of problem-solving skills, emotional regulation, and social understanding. Gray asserts that giving children more autonomy could reverse declining mental health trends and better prepare them for adulthood. In parenting, autonomy means allowing children to make choices and take responsibility for their decisions, while assuring them of unconditional love. Your love for your kids shouldn't depend on how many rebounds, hits, or tackles they make. If we adopted a more autonomous approach to youth sports, children might be less judgmental of their peers and less likely to cry after making the slightest error under the pressure of the crowd. We might see fewer children throwing tantrums with equipment in dugouts. Parents, too, could find more joy watching their kids simply enjoy the sport with friends.

Generation Z faces unprecedented mental health challenges, with anxiety now the most common disorder among today's youth. Research shows that more than 70 percent of Gen Z reports experiencing anxiety or depression, and student-athletes are especially vulnerable as they juggle the dual pressures of academics and sports. Coaches are uniquely positioned to recognize these struggles and to create environments that support both performance and well-being. This means encouraging open communication, weaving mental health awareness into athletic programs, and connecting athletes with professional resources when necessary.

Above all, we must prioritize well-being over performance. Winning games will always matter, but it should never define a young athlete's worth. The true opportunity lies in preparing them for life beyond the playing field, and teaching resilience, teamwork, and confidence.

A BROADER PERSPECTIVE ON MENTAL HEALTH

Beyond the sports field, mental health remains a pressing issue in today's society. Many individuals are just one setback away from financial instability or homelessness. During my eight-year hiatus from education, my wife and I built a successful residential cleaning business in North Texas. While Sarah is the true driving force behind our company's growth, my focus on sales, marketing, and hiring taught me invaluable lessons about the state of our workforce and the challenges people face.

One of the most eye-opening experiences has been navigating the hiring process. We often sift through 100 applications to find one qualified candidate. While we prioritize heart, compassion, and work ethic, we frequently encounter applicants who lack basic motivation or professionalism. Some miss interviews entirely, arrive late, or show up unprepared. This has revealed a deeper issue: many people are struggling, often one bad situation away from a crisis. The older I get, the more I recognize the complexity of these struggles. Many of those standing on street corners with cardboard signs are not lazy. They are people wrestling with trauma, bad decisions, or circumstances beyond their control. They are someone's loved ones, and their situations reflect the mental health challenges that are increasingly pervasive in our society.

THE ROLE OF COACHES IN SHAPING THE WORLD

As I reflect on these experiences, I can not help but worry about the long-term impact we are having on today's youth. By failing to nurture their love for sports and by overlooking their mental health needs, we risk leaving them broken and disconnected. Coaches have the power to make a transformative difference, but only if we rise to the challenge and adapt to the evolving needs of our players.

Coaching Generation Z athletes requires balancing tradition with innovation, demands a willingness to embrace new challenges, and to refine our strategies to support their growth. Many student-athletes now struggle with balancing academics, sports, and personal commitments, making time management a key focus. By prioritizing their overall development, we can prepare these young athletes not just for sports, but for life.

As I guide my players, I am reminded of the verses in Philippians 4:6-7: *"Do not be anxious about anything, but in every situation, by prayer and petition, with thanksgiving, present your requests to God. And the peace of God, which transcends all understanding, will guard your hearts and your minds in Christ Jesus."* These words offer a reminder that even in the face of challenges, peace and resilience are possible. It is time for all of us, parents, coaches, and communities, to come together and recognize the sincere influence we have on the next generation. Let's ensure that our athletes leave the field not just as better players, but as stronger, healthier individuals ready to take on the world.

BUILDING STRONG RELATIONSHIPS AND LEVERAGING INFLUENCE

Great football coaches understand their role goes beyond drawing up plays or mastering the X's and O's. They are mentors, leaders, and role models who uniquely shape players' lives. For many younger coaches, however, building deep, face-to-face connections can feel less natural. Having grown up in a digital-first era where screens often replaced direct human interaction, they may lack the interpersonal skills earlier generations relied on. We must intentionally address this by teaching the importance of effective human connection.

Today, the need for strong, intentional relationships has never been greater. Trust, resilience, and commitment are not accidents; they are cultivated through meaningful human connection. Dale Carnegie's timeless principles in *How to Win Friends and Influence People* remain just as relevant, offering simple yet powerful strategies for earning trust and fostering understanding. That book shaped my early career and taught me how to lead with compassion and purpose.

To the next generation of coaches and parents guiding today's athletes: recognize the gap in connection, rise to the challenge, and embrace the opportunity to grow. Building strong bonds with your players is the foundation of effective leadership. Such skill, every great coach should master.

KEY LESSONS FROM DALE CARNEGIE FOR COACHES

1. BE A GREAT LISTENER

Carnegie emphasizes the value of listening over talking, a lesson every coach should take to heart. Coaches need to create an environment where athletes feel safe to express themselves. Truly hearing your players not only strengthens team dynamics but also shows them they are valued. Take the time to listen, whether they are sharing their passion for the game or something entirely unrelated to sports. You may be the only person who makes eye contact and shows genuine interest in what matters to them. That connection, however small, can have a lifelong impact. Even if a player spends only a couple of years in your program, the memories they carry should be positive, meaningful, and lasting.

2. SHOW GENUINE INTEREST

Take time to learn about your players' lives beyond the field. Every athlete has a unique story, challenges, and aspirations. If you are not genuinely curious about the individuals on your team, you are missing an opportunity to make a difference, and you might not truly deserve the title of "coach." A sincere effort to understand your players helps you tailor guidance and create a supportive environment.

3. RESPECT INDIVIDUAL DIFFERENCES

Acknowledging where each player is in their journey is critical to their development. A beginner requires a different approach than a seasoned athlete. For example, a struggling youth baseball player may benefit more from learning how to lay down a bunt than from swinging for home runs. Celebrate those small victories just as much as the big ones, because for that player, it represents a genuine moment of pride. Respect is not just about recognizing talent; it is about meeting each player where they are and giving them the tools to succeed.

4. OFFER SINCERE APPRECIATION

Recognizing effort and celebrating milestones, no matter how small, boosts players' confidence and fosters a sense of belonging. A simple "thank you" can go a long way. Thank your players for giving their best effort, picking up equipment after practice, or consistently showing up on time for morning sessions. Every player, regardless of skill level, should feel valued for their contributions. As a coach, your job is to ensure each athlete knows they are an important part of the bigger picture.

5. REMEMBER NAMES AND DETAILS

Calling players by their names and remembering details about their lives shows that you value them as individuals. A warm greeting or thoughtful comment helps build connections and sets a positive tone. If you struggle with names, make an effort to learn them—it is worth it. Knowing your players by name demonstrates care and can significantly impact their sense of belonging.

As a coach, you don't have to rely solely on memory, especially when working with many kids. Use creative ways to learn their names during the first week of practice. For example, have players say their names at the end of ladder drills, write their names on tape on their helmets, or simply ask when you forget. Players do not expect perfection - they will appreciate the effort and be happy to help you remember because their name matters to them.

6. LEAD WITH COMPASSION

Compassion builds an environment where players feel supported and accepted. Every athlete has something to contribute, and it is the coach's role to nurture that potential. Encourage players to grow in their own way and remind them that their value is not defined solely by performance. Dr. Gabor Maté emphasizes that disconnection from one's authentic self, often formed in response to early childhood struggles, can hinder emotional growth. As a coach, you have the chance to create a space where young athletes feel accepted for who they truly are, fostering both personal and athletic development.

By applying these principles, coaches can inspire and motivate players, instilling not only athletic skills but also life lessons that extend far beyond the game. Genuine relationships are the foundation of effective coaching. When you invest in your players with compassion, respect, and care, you equip them with tools and memories that last a lifetime.

Coaching is a rewarding journey, and one worth mastering.

THE LOST BOYS OF YOUTH SPORTS

There is a reason the story of Peter Pan continues to resonate across generations. In its simplest form, it tells the story of a boy who refused to grow up, holding on to the wild magic of childhood in a world determined to take it away. In Neverland, children could fly, imagine, play, and lead their own adventures. That spirit of wonder, where dreams of magical places and hidden treasures come alive, is something we must cherish and protect. Every child deserves the freedom to explore, dream, and play, at least until the world inevitably challenges their innocence. Today, however, that freedom is disappearing for many young athletes.

When we label a nine-year-old as elite, reduce their childhood to stats and rankings, or train the joy out of the game, we are stealing their Neverland. We are asking them to grow up too quickly, to perform like adults, and to carry pressures they were never meant to bear. Let us be honest. No nine-year-old wants to play eighty baseball games in a single season. No seven-year-old naturally wants to hurl their body into another child during a modified version of the Oklahoma drill in youth football practice. Most kids that age would much rather play tag, chase bugs, or simply have fun. Yet here they are, standing in 100-degree heat, being barked at by parents who spend more time obsessing over their "playbooks" than fishing with their kids.

Here is the truth: your child does not care nearly as much as you think they do. And while we are on the subject of playbooks, let me just say this; yes, a well-drawn play can help kids understand the basics of the game, but this obsession with creating overly complicated playbooks has gotten out of hand. Here's another secret about playbooks: they don't actually exist—except in movies. That 400-page "master plan playbook" you imagine Nick Saban keeps locked in a vault? It does not exist. So, keep it simple. If you are coaching youth football or baseball, you need maybe two run plays and two pass plays. That is enough. Quit overcomplicating the game, because in doing so, you are stealing something precious from your kids without even realizing it.

"All children, except one, grow up." — J.M. Barrie, *Peter Pan*

In too many youth sports environments, kids are not just growing up, they are being forced into adulthood far too soon, both emotionally and physically. The game becomes a transaction instead of a playground. The childhood they should enjoy on the field gets hijacked by adult anxieties, overzealous coaching, and misplaced priorities. The right coach, however, can change everything.

A good coach protects joy. He keeps the pressure off. He allows kids to stay for just a little while longer. Childhood is fleeting, and once it is gone, you can not get it back. In a world where so many children already face the challenges of fatherlessness or other hardships, youth sports should be a safe haven - a place where the innocence of being young is restored, not stripped away.

Too many of us have forgotten the magic of Peter Pan's Neverland. Our kids have not, and they deserve to hold on to that magic for as long as they can.

As parents, we often forget how important it is to tell our kids we are proud of them, no matter the outcome of the game. Somewhere along the way, we have bought into the idea that hiring specialists to help our kids achieve greatness is essential. This mindset is unrealistic and often counterproductive. We see it everywhere: in sports, education, and even in the friendships we nudge our kids toward, sometimes based on our own connections as parents.

Take youth sports, for example. Many parents pay for coaches to hone their seven-year-old's technique, believing it will lead to success. But at that age, what kids need most is not technical perfection, it is a love for the game. My grandmother, who was always strapped for cash, taught me this lesson in the simplest way. When I was about ten or eleven, she would take me to the Putt-Putt batting cages in Arlington, TX before a game. She did not say a word about my swing. She would just sit behind the cage, smoking a cigarette, while I smashed the ball as hard as I could, imagining I was going to break the machine. There was no over-coaching, no nitpicking, just pure fun and effort. Those moments stayed with me.

Too often today, we are over-teaching and over-coaching our kids, focusing on drills and techniques instead of helping them fall in love with the sport. If we shifted our focus to fostering joy, effort, and the very basics of the game, we would be building a stronger foundation for their growth, not just as athletes, but as people.

I love motivating young people. A few years ago, at one of my son's t-ball practices, some other dads were brainstorming ways to help our team improve at hitting. While their intentions were good, their suggestions for hitting drills were far too technical for five and six-year-olds. They discussed concepts like rotational versus linear swings, but kids that age can't grasp those mechanics. If it is not fun for a five-year-old, it does not matter to them. No five-year-old will ever understand complex hitting theory, but they do, however, understand the importance of ice cream. That day, I brought a slightly deflated soccer ball and had the players at my station swing as hard as they could to hit it as far as possible. They knew the player who hit it the furthest would win an ice cream sandwich. It was simple, fun, and encouraged good habits without the pressure of strict technical rules. The kids were swinging out of their shoes and having a blast! I'm no major league coach, but I've played enough baseball to know that creating a fun environment is far more impactful than the over-engineered drills you see online. Laugh all you want, but I would take a group of kids motivated by the promise of an ice cream sandwich over a hyper-trained, technical team any day. They'd have more fun, and years later, they'd remember those games and that ice cream with far more joy than an over-coached player wishing they had the ice cream sandwiches my team enjoyed on the next field over!

Beyond sports, we have become selfish in how we approach parenting, and it is hurting our kids. Many parents push their children toward prestigious colleges, believing that it guarantees wealth, success, or happiness. Too many of us have forgotten that happiness does not come from a degree. It comes from living a life aligned with your values. As a coach and as a parent, it is our job to guide our kids toward joy and fulfillment, not to outsource their success. Not every child needs a college degree to thrive. Kids should understand that careers like plumbing or owning an HVAC business can provide a stable and lucrative income. In a world where fewer people have hands-on skills and rely heavily on service industries, these professions are more valuable than ever. The world needs happy people in fulfilling careers more than it needs a checklist of credentials.

This shift in mindset could address broader societal issues as well. A significant factor contributing to the growing homelessness crisis is our misplaced perceptions of value and success. We have failed to teach young people the fundamentals of self-worth, accountability, and resilience. Instead, we mock what is right and protect what is wrong, turning a blind eye to timeless values. The Bible reminds us that these challenges are not new. Evil has always appeared in many forms, yet truth has always been there to guide us. The reality is, each of us is uniquely gifted with distinct talents and insights.

So, what should we teach our kids? Let them enjoy their childhood while showing them how to build meaningful friendships and what true friends say, do, and stand for. Teach them basic financial skills, such as the realities of living paycheck to paycheck. Be their safe space, the person they trust to share their thoughts and fears. Show them the value of hard work, but also the importance of love, joy, and play. Let them see what a healthy, loving relationship looks like at home. Celebrate others' successes and teach them when to hold their tongue, but also when to speak out in the face of injustice. Help them identify fake friends and understand the superficial nature of shallow relationships. Encourage them to find comfort in a church pew, to brush their teeth, and to laugh when they spot that first armpit hair. Teach them the pitfalls of too much screen time and the importance of questioning what they read online, especially with the rise of artificial intelligence.

Remind them that perfection is unattainable and that it is okay to be goofy sometimes. Teach them the difference between a kolache and a pig in a blanket. Take them fishing, show them how to light a fire, and help them roast a sausage over a fire pit wrapped in a flour tortilla with a hint of mustard. Teach them how to win, and more importantly, how to lose gracefully. These are the moments that matter. These are the lessons that last.

If we focus on these essentials, we'll not only raise well-rounded kids but also help create a future filled with happier, more resilient individuals. Let's step back, simplify, and give them the tools they truly need to thrive.

IGNORING THE WISDOM OF THE GREATS

We often celebrate the greatest moments in sports history, reminiscing about legendary achievements and watching highlight reels like seasoned experts. When it comes to youth sports and parenting, however, we frequently overlook the advice of those who truly understand the game, the very athletes who have reached the pinnacle of their fields. Even worse, we sometimes do exactly the opposite of what they recommend.

Pay close attention to the words of some of the greatest athletes and advocates in sports. Their words offer valuable insights into how we can guide our kids more effectively in sports today.

1. Cal Ripken Jr.

"Let your kids fall in love with the game on their own. Your job isn't to push—it's to support and encourage."

2. Bo Jackson

"We're wearing kids out with year-round sports and overcoaching. Let them be kids. Let them rest. Let them play."

3. Michael Jordan

"You have to let kids choose their own path. I never pushed my kids to be me—I wanted them to be themselves."

4. Jeff Frye *(former MLB player and advocate against poor coaching)*

"Dads, stop acting like you're coaching Game 7 of the World Series in Little League. Let the kids learn and have fun."

5. Steve Harvey *(as a parent and mentor in youth sports)*

"It ain't your life to live again through your kid. Let them mess up, learn, grow. Cheer—but don't control."

6. Gilbert Arenas

"Parents trying to coach from the stands are the problem. Let the coach coach. Let the kid play."

7. Shaquille O'Neal

"I tell my kids: I made my name. Now you make yours. I don't pressure them to be me—I just support them."

8. Tom Brady

"Too many parents think their 10-year-old has to be perfect. Just let them enjoy it. Fun comes before success."

9. Kobe Bryant

"Youth sports aren't about winning at age 8. They're about learning, failing, and finding joy in the process."

10. Aaron Rodgers

"If you're screaming at your kid after the game, you've already lost. Make the car ride home a safe place."

11. Steve Kerr

"The stands are for cheering, not coaching. Parents should clap, not yell instructions. It messes kids up."

12. J.J. Watt

"If you're yelling at your kid, the ref, or another parent from the stands—you're doing youth sports wrong."

13. Chris Paul

"Let coaches coach. Let kids play. Parents should support, not overshadow, their children's experience."

14. Derek Jeter

"Kids don't need pressure. They need passion. Support their love for the game, not your expectations."

15. Peyton Manning

"Encouragement is more powerful than critique. Kids remember how you made them feel more than what you said."

16. Charles Barkley

"Adults have ruined youth sports. Stop yelling. Stop pressuring. Just let the damn kids play."

17. Serena Williams

"I wasn't pushed—I was guided. There's a difference. Parents should know when to step back and just believe."

18. Tony Dungy

"Sports are an incredible tool for character, but only when adults focus on more than just the scoreboard."

19. Tim Tebow

"It's not about wins. It's about who your child is becoming through the process. Don't miss that."

20. Andre Agassi

"I hated tennis as a kid because I wasn't playing for me. I was playing for my dad. No child should feel that."

THE DANGER OF OVER-PARENTING IN YOUTH SPORTS

Despite the wisdom of countless great minds, we often ignore their advice, falling instead into harmful habits like over-criticism, over-scheduling, and micromanagement. Comedian Theo Von captures the danger of this approach perfectly:

"When you keep criticizing your kids, they don't stop loving you. They stop loving themselves."

This mindset is especially prevalent in today's youth sports culture, where a damaging myth persists: the belief that a child can be "elite" by the age of nine. While the label may sound impressive, it is both misleading and harmful.

If you take away just one message from this chapter, let it be this: The most important thing you can say to your child after a game, a recital, or even catching a big fish is, "I'm so proud of you!"

We do not say this enough, and we need to say it far more often. When you tell your child you are proud of them, you send a powerful message: they are enough, independent of how they performed.

Be proud of your kids for trying. Be proud of them for being silly. Be proud when they show courage, when they are a good teammate, or when they simply try something new. Let them feel your pride all the time, and stop focusing on constant corrections.

Your pride in them does not have to be earned. Rather, it should just be felt. That simple shift can make all the difference.

THE MYTH OF "ELITE ATHLETES" AT NINE YEARS OLD

Performance coach and author Steve Magness offers a blunt reality check:

"There is no such thing as an elite athlete at nine years old. But club coaches and other parents keep insisting that if you don't treat them like one, they will fall behind and never be able to catch up."

This belief has become so widespread that it is often disguised as responsibility or sacrifice. Parents are told their child needs more repetitions, private training, tournaments, and fewer distractions such as other sports, hobbies, or even rest.

But the data and experience tell a very different story. Magness, who has studied long-term athletic performance, warns that early labeling does more harm than good. Instead of fostering confidence, it creates pressure. Instead of cultivating a love for the game, it often leads to burnout.

Magness stresses that "When kids are told they are elite too early, it creates a fear of losing that identity. They start playing not to lose status, instead of playing to learn and grow."

The consequences are alarming. Studies show that up to seventy percent of children quit organized sports by age thirteen. One of the most common reasons? "It is not fun anymore." Fun disappears when the game becomes a job, especially a job that starts in third grade.

THE HIDDEN CHALLENGE IN YOUTH SPORTS

As parents and coaches, it is important to ask ourselves some tough questions: Are we truly guiding our children, or are we projecting our own ambitions onto them? Are we encouraging exploration and discovery, or are we forcing them into performance-driven paths before they are ready?

The reality is that elite performance is not determined at age nine. It is built over years of growth, effort, and experience. At that age, children do not need labels or brands. They need freedom, the freedom to play, to fail, to explore, and to discover what brings them joy. They need adults who protect that joy, not those who try to profit from it.

We can benefit by taking the wisdom of great athletes and coaches to heart. Sports should be a tool for fun, learning, and personal growth, not a source of pressure or misplaced parental ambition. As Tim Tebow wisely said, it is not about the wins, it is about who our kids are becoming. Let us not lose sight of that.

THE DADDY BALL RANT

Youth sports should be about growth, teamwork, and fostering a love for the game. Unfortunately, an all-too-common dynamic disrupts this ideal: the influence of so-called "Daddy Ball" coaches. These individuals prioritize winning above all else, chasing short-term success at the expense of player development and team cohesion. While their initial focus on winning may make them appear effective, their true nature becomes clear when challenges arise, such as team conflicts or a streak of losses.

"Daddy Ball" coaches often show favoritism, prioritizing certain players, frequently their own children or those of close friends, while neglecting the growth of others. This favoritism undermines team dynamics, as they excessively praise certain players while dismissing or criticizing those less skilled. A key flaw of this approach is their inability to assess talent objectively, often making decisions driven by personal agendas rather than the team's best interests. This behavior frequently stems from a desire to relive their own unfulfilled athletic aspirations through their children. As Mike Matheny notes in *The Dad Coach*, "Too many dads are coaching to build up their own egos or to make up for what they missed in their own athletic careers, rather than to help every kid on the team grow and improve."

The impact of "Daddy Ball" often extends beyond youth leagues into high school sports, where some parents pressure schools to replace experienced coaches if their child does not receive enough playing time. These situations often arise because the child lacks essential traits like mental toughness, work ethic, or sportsmanship, qualities coaches rely upon to build successful teams. Unfortunately, the focus on catering to individual egos detracts from the overall development of the team and its players.

Having experienced this firsthand, I firmly believe that true coaching is rooted in selflessness. Great coaches prioritize the team's success over personal pride, fostering growth in every player, not just a select few. Matheny's insights highlight the importance of intentional, character-driven coaching that values long-term development over short-term victories. Ultimately, the role of any coach should be to guide young athletes toward becoming better players and better people.

Some coaches inadvertently extinguish young athletes' passion for sports, particularly those on the fringes, often playing a significant role in ending their athletic journeys prematurely. They overlook the tantrums of favored players while unfairly overreacting to those they see as "non-contributors," simply because these players are easier to single out. Confronting a star player is rarely an option, as they fear losing them and jeopardizing their winning streak. Here is the truth: eternity does not care about your winning streak. Years from now, most people will not remember how dominant your team was. What players will remember is how you made them feel and how your actions shaped their experience.

I urge all coaches to rekindle the joy of sports in their players, a joy that should never be defined by stats. Too often, those numbers reflect little more than the bias of the parent recording them. A coach's real purpose is to cultivate love for the game, not inflate egos or cater to favoritism.

Consider the kinds of comments that echo through little league dugouts: *"Alright, we're at the best part of our lineup, let's score some runs!"* To the coach, it may sound motivational. But to the rest of the team, the message is clear: *you're just tolerated.* These are the moments when baseball still holds its magic for young players, filled with hope and possibility. Yet it is often parents, sometimes unintentionally, who dim that light. In trying to elevate their own child as the next star, they teach their kids to look down on teammates and dismiss the dreams of others along the way.

I know that as a dad, I have sometimes been seen as a nuisance in the dugout. People notice that I pay attention, that I care about things being done fairly. Too often, though, my intentions are misjudged. They assume I am just like the rest, pulling strings for special treatment. What they do not realize is that I am there for all the kids, not just my own. I care deeply about the role coaches play, especially in shaping impressionable young minds.

I will also admit I am not perfect. In the past, I have said and done things to coaches and fellow parents that I regret. I have been unfair at times. But I have worked hard to grow more patient and more understanding, and I know I have changed. Still, the issues I see in youth sports today, like favoritism, selfishness, and misplaced priorities, remain systemic problems that deserve attention.

I believe that all children should face challenges, even when they are difficult. These moments are essential for growth. When I notice "daddy ball" affecting their joy, I approach the topic with care. I never compare my kids to others or insist they deserve more playing time. Instead, I speak up only when I see them genuinely hurt by a coach's behavior, whether it is selfishness, unfairness, or simply a lack of awareness about how to treat kids. Sometimes, it is not even intentional; it is just a coach overpromising and underdelivering.

Coaches hold immense power. They can inspire or discourage, uplift or tear down. Each of us who answer to "Hey, Coach!" must understand the lasting impact they have, not only on the scoreboard but on the hearts and minds of the kids who look up to them.

When I describe certain coaches as having a "win at all costs" mentality, I am referring to those who push the rules to their limits, even when they are already leading by 12 runs. They fixate on point differentials or the optics of a close win instead of giving another player the chance to pitch the final inning, an opportunity that could become an unforgettable memory. This mindset is not only disheartening but also misguided.

When I use the term "daddy ball," I am not just talking about fathers who favor their own children. I mean any coach who fails to act with fairness and integrity, neglecting to treat players with the respect they deserve. If I have applied the term too broadly, I apologize. Still, these issues are widespread in youth sports, across both boys' and girls' teams. Watching football from the sidelines, I often recall a simple yet powerful truth I once heard: there are two types of coaches in this world, those who genuinely care about every child on the team and those who do not. I cannot remember where I first came across this saying, but its message resonates deeply with me.

I have no tolerance for the latter. It is heartbreaking that such coaches exist, tarnishing the reputation of those who embody what coaching should truly be.

On the football sidelines, it is easy to spot coaches who lack genuine care for their players by the phrases they use: "Do as you were taught," "I didn't teach you to do that," or "Nobody is blocking, nobody is doing anything." From the stands, however, it is much harder to distinguish them from coaches who are fully dedicated. Even the most committed coaches can express frustration in similar ways.

What makes this distinction so challenging is the nature of football itself. The sport demands relentless effort, often five days of practice a week, with coaches working six or seven to prepare. The real work happens during those long hours on the field and in the locker room, where relationships are built, lessons are taught, and players are prepared. Yet these moments of dedication are invisible to fans watching from the stands on Friday nights.

A fully committed coach and one who has done the bare minimum can appear indistinguishable from the outside. To spectators, both may look equally engaged. The true measure of a coach lies not in what is seen during the game, but in the unseen effort invested in players behind the scenes.

These are the same coaches who, on the football field, prioritize the most athletic kid over the one who listens and applies instruction, chasing short-term results. They favor players whose parents are louder or more influential, regardless of actual talent. They reprimand a player for mistakes they were never properly coached to avoid, using that as a reason to bench them. Instead of acknowledging effort or teaching through errors, these coaches resort to harsh criticism and sideline the player. This approach is not only frustrating but fundamentally flawed.

Rather than focusing on developing their players, some coaches spend their energy cultivating relationships with influential individuals to secure their own positions. They surround themselves with staff who either share their lack of initiative or blindly follow poor leadership. As a result, the entire coaching staff perpetuates an unhealthy culture, mistreating players and undermining team performance. The outcome is predictable: frequent losses, close games that should have been easy wins, and embarrassing defeats that expose their incompetence.

During these moments of failure, the cracks in leadership become painfully clear. Players throw helmets in frustration, coaches shout and slam their headsets, and kids stand unnoticed on the sidelines, desperate for acknowledgment. Some players fake injuries to escape the chaos, skip practices, and eventually lose all respect for their so-called coaches. This toxic cycle erodes team morale and betrays the very essence of what coaching should be.

Programs led by this style of leadership lack substance and depth. While these coaches may form relationships with players, the connections are surface-level and fail to make a lasting impact. They may dedicate weekends to the team, but their efforts rarely translate into meaningful results. They claim to care about their athletes yet fail to check in after injuries from the night before. They say they know their players, but they cannot share even the most basic insights into their home lives.

At parent meetings, the pseudo coaches emphasize the value of playing multiple sports, but later discourage participation in spring activities for fear it might interfere with their preferred sport. They shy away from praising fellow coaches, worried it will diminish their own standing. Intimidated by peers with stronger principles, they disregard the influence of quality coaching. Ironically, the very kind of coaching that likely inspired them to pursue the profession in the first place.

Though aware of their flaws, self centered coaches refuse to confront them, allowing ego to overshadow any genuine love for the game. In doing so, they lose sight of the true purpose of competition. Instead of teaching players how to compete with integrity and resilience, they reduce everything to winning and losing. They leave no room to develop character or instill values. This approach diminishes the essence of coaching and strips away the opportunity to prepare players for both sports and life.

These "pretend" coaches show little regard for their players' behavior outside the game. They ignore poor conduct in classrooms and hallways, deflecting blame onto teachers for misbehavior. Quick to point fingers when things go wrong, they rarely acknowledge the contributions of others, even when victories come by chance. When outcoached, they avoid shaking hands, misinterpreting the competitive spirit of opposing teams as disrespect. They teach their players to disdain tougher, grittier opponents, confusing tenacity with being "dirty." In doing so, they fail to instill respect for competition, missing the vital lesson that true respect can and should be shown, even in victory.

Let me be clear: I love coaches. I love the role they play, not just as professionals but also as parents, mentors, and leaders. That is why I am, and always will be, a critic of anyone who carries the title of "coach" yet fails to uphold the responsibilities it demands. To me, there are only two types of coaches: those who put kids first and those who do not. There is no gray area. It is the ultimate rivalry. You are either one of the good ones or you are not. You are Team A or Team B, Team Blue or Team Red. So pick your side.

A year and a half before I fully committed to finishing this book, I shared my draft with a developmental editor for feedback. Their insights were incredibly valuable, highlighting areas that needed more work, some I was already aware of, and others I was grateful they pointed out. However, one piece of feedback stood out: they mentioned that parts of my writing felt "too pointed" or "unnecessarily confrontational." While I respect their perspective, I want to be clear: I didn't change a single word in response to that critique.

It is okay to have strong beliefs. It is okay to stand up for what truly matters. I understand that my views may not resonate with everyone, especially those whose experiences differ from mine. But I firmly believe the coaching profession is worth fighting for, and I stand behind every word I've written. My goal is to embody what I call an "Armageddon Coach" for myself, my kids, the players I mentor, and the communities I serve. I want to honor the coaches who shaped me, those who did the job the right way and made it look effortless. While we all have room to grow, including myself, we must hold onto the values that define our calling.

We can, and must do better. For the kids. For the communities we serve. For the future of coaching. Let's rise to the occasion, uphold the ideals of this profession, and embody the values that coaching truly deserves.

COACH'S REFLECTION:

- Are your decisions as a coach strengthening the unity and integrity of the coaching community, or are they contributing to the challenges you aim to address?

- Do you regularly assess how your career aligns with your personal values, family priorities, and long-term aspirations?

- Is your focus on the growth and well-being of your players and colleagues, or are you primarily driven by personal ambition?

- In moments of difficulty, do you stand firm for what is right, or do you avoid conflict for the sake of convenience?

- What lasting impact do you want to leave, not only for your players but for the entire coaching community?

Reflect deeply on these questions and consider how your actions reflect the values you believe in each day.

CHAPTER 12

GOD IS REAL

Looking back on the journey that has led me to where I am today, I remember when I first recited the Lord's Prayer as a football player. It was during my time as an Ennis Lion, and truth be told, I played countless games before I finally learned all the words. Before each game, I'd bow my head with the team, mumble along, occasionally catching a word I knew, and faithfully end with *"Lead us not into temptation but deliver us from evil."* I'd stumble through a bit more before finally reaching, "For the kingdom, the power, and the glory, forever and ever. Amen."

Moments like these taught me that football is about more than just plays. Football is about passion. Football is a sacred connection, a spiritual bond forged on the fields of Texas, where high school football remains pure, untamed, and deeply meaningful.

I want to share another story from my journey of faith. In my early coaching days, I worked at Palmer ISD alongside Coach Clif White. When I first arrived, I did not know him, but I quickly discovered that he was an absolute joy to be around. Clif represented everything I cherish about the coaching profession. He embodied what it meant to live and love like Jesus. At the time, I was only 24 years old, and my relationship with God was not as strong as it is today.

To know Clif was to love him. His infectious smile and vibrant spirit made him unforgettable. He was a delightful mix of movie quotes, a love for food, and endless sports enthusiasm, always capable of brightening your day. What stood out most, though, was his unwavering love for God, which he expressed openly both in the coach's office and among his players.

I spent only a year at Palmer, but like many coaches, I built friendships with my colleagues through the camaraderie of football season. After I left, Clif and I did not stay in regular contact. Still, whenever we crossed paths at a coaching clinic or elsewhere, it felt like no time had passed. That is the nature of the coaching world: once you move to another school, maintaining connections becomes difficult under the demands of a new job and the pressures of life in general.

Then, on May 28, 2022, I came across a Facebook post from Clif's wife, Meagan, which read:

"It is time to tell you all what has been thrown to us. Clif has been diagnosed with stage 4 Urachal Cancer which is extremely rare. Less than 1 in a million. It developed from his umbilical cord when he was in the womb.

Dr said it has spread to his lymph nodes and is concerned about a small mass in his right lung. The oncologist we saw says he is not the best person to attack this rare case, so he is referring us to MD Anderson in Houston. We already have that process started.

Clif is my earth, air, fire and water. He is everything. There is no time to put a question mark where God has put a period. I have declared war with this and God has assembled us the most amazing army of friends and family to walk through the pits of hell with us . For that we are eternally grateful.

Cancer has picked the wrong husband, father, and friend to mess with. We have the full armor of God to equip us for this fight. If it's a fight cancer wants, it's a fight it's going to get.

We request that you all strap up and fight on your knees with us in prayer for my husband and our family. Prayer is powerful. Lift your hands high and scream for healing, strength, courage, mountain moving, sea parting and stone rolling power in the name of Jesus."

I wanted you to read the post to understand how I processed everything that unfolded. That evening, after coming across the Facebook post, my wife Sarah and I had been arguing over something so trivial that I can not even recall what it was. It was just one of those chaotic, stressful nights that life occasionally throws your way. But, I was quickly humbled with the facebook post above. As I read the post, though, everything else faded. I broke down in tears, a rare occurrence for me, as I'm not someone who cries easily. But at that moment, I wept. I wept for myself, for Clif and his family, and for my own children. The floodgates opened, and I could not hold back the tears. My heart felt heavy, burdened by an exhaustion I could not ignore. It was as though I was surrendering to something far greater than myself, a vulnerability I had never felt before. At that moment, I realized I could no longer navigate this journey of life alone.

When I looked up information on stage 4 urachal cancer, the outlook was devastating. Google offered grim statistics, painting a picture of a life expectancy capped at two years. But this was Clif we were talking about, and I knew one thing without a doubt: this cancer was in for a battle. Clif's resilience and unyielding spirit were unmatched, driven by a heart full of fight.

Five months later, we laid Clif to rest, and once again, my tears flowed freely. Over the years, many coaches and mentors have shaped me, most connected through football or other sports. Each left a significant mark on my life and faith, but the five months of Clif's battle with cancer felt profoundly different, almost surreal. During that time, I witnessed something extraordinary: Clif coming to terms with his mortality. For someone like me, who was not saved back then, this was a concept I struggled to grasp, but through Clif, I began to understand how acceptance was possible. His inexorable faith in God gave him an unshakable peace, a belief that, in the end, everything would be okay.

I also watched his wife, Meagan, face those months with incredible strength, an almost superhuman resilience sustained by divine support. She created a Facebook group to keep everyone updated, as so many people were praying for their family and wanted to know how they were doing. Through her posts, she allowed all of us to be part of their journey. Whether she realized it or not, those updates had a profound effect, not just on me, but on everyone who followed their story during those five months.

I often found myself in awe, wondering how she continued to share, to post, and to quote Scripture, even in their hardest moments. Her words flowed steadily, like a stream of hope. And Clif, despite his battle, held on to peace until the very end. It was incredible to witness and a true testament to the promise that God will never leave you and will never place you in a situation you cannot endure without His presence. The difference between Clif, Meagan, and their children and where I was at that time was striking: they knew this truth deeply, while I was only beginning to see it unfold in real time.

Later in this chapter, I reflect on the tragedy of my childhood, when I lost my sister Katlyn. Looking back now, I can see that even then I was surrounded by divine support, though I did not recognize it. Witnessing Clif and Meagan's faith was transformative for me. It became a powerful catalyst, drawing me closer to a faith and perspective I had never truly understood until then. Their journey was a testament to God's steadfast presence, and I carry that lesson with me to this day.

A number of years ago, I joined a Bible study group with a remarkable group of older gentlemen who showed me incredible kindness. During our time together, we studied a book called *The Red Sea Rules* by Robert J. Morgan. If you haven't read it, I can not recommend it enough. Truthfully, I'm not even sure if Meagan has read the book, but I'm sharing it with you because that same group of men encouraged me to share this story with Meagan and her kids. They believed it was important for them to hear it from me and understand just how much love and inspiration came from simply knowing Clif.

Meagan truly exemplified the principles outlined in *The Red Sea*

Rules. She crafted a beautiful, heartfelt plan for Clif, herself, and their children, the one that reflected the wisdom of the book's lessons. After enduring tragedy, she embodied these teachings so deeply that I hope they resonate with you as well. Perhaps one day, you will share these lessons with someone in your life, maybe even a player, and help them navigate their own challenges with hope and strength.

- God places you where you are meant to be.
- Recognize your adversaries, but focus on God.
- Pray consistently.
- Remain calm and confident, allowing God time to act.
- See your current crisis as a faith-builder for the future.
- When uncertain, take the next logical step with faith.
- Envision God's encompassing presence.
- Trust God to deliver in His own unique way.

Witnessing this unfold transformed my faith, moving me from simply believing in God to truly knowing He exists. To Meagan, Maverick, and Riggins: your dad's story is extraordinary. It is the most powerful story I know, and whether he realized it or not, his unwavering faith and deep love for God guided me to find my own. I know how much he loves you all. Stay strong and faithful. He was, through and through, an "Armageddon Coach."

That moment also marked a turning point for my family, shifting our path back into God's embrace. I am here to tell you that God is real. As coaches from all walks of life, and from all faiths and denominations, we share an incredible opportunity and responsibility to mentor young leaders while standing firm as pillars of strength in our communities. Now more than ever, we must defend our values boldly, or risk losing them entirely. Call it a conspiracy if you will, but I believe true evil, in whatever form it manifests in your community, has recognized the profound influence we have on our players. And it will stop at nothing to sever that connection.

I have seen it happen. Too many good coaches, men of integrity who change lives for the better, have fallen victim to this evil we all know exists in some way. And if we fail to act, if we fail to protect one another, the dedicated few who remain will eventually leave the profession altogether. We cannot let that happen.

This is a call to action. Let us strengthen our community of coaches and recommit ourselves to the truth and values that shape the lives of so many. As Maximus said, "At my signal, unleash hell." With courage and leadership, we must face the challenges ahead and lead with conviction. The stakes are too high to do anything less.

My purpose is clear, shaped by experiences with people like Clif White and Katlyn. It has also been quietly influenced by people in my life, like my friend Matt Newman, who gave me my first Bible on our way to San Saba for a weekend hunting trip.As coaches, I pray we focus on the good in a world where negativity is so often amplified. I ask that God helps us see the opportunities we have to make a difference, even amidst challenges like NIL controversies, frequent player transfers chasing greener pastures, and the constant changes reshaping our profession.

Our mission is to plant seeds of faith and leadership. Seeds that may take years to grow, but they will grow. Sometimes it takes 20 years or more for those seeds to flourish, but someone must plant them. As coaches, we are uniquely positioned to sow these seeds, especially in today's ever-evolving society. The role of a coach has transformed over the years and will continue to do so, but the core mission remains timeless: to build God's army and serve as champions of faith and leadership, preserving the integrity of our profession and the profound generational impact it carries.There's no better scripture to illustrate a coach's relationship with a player than Job 29:12–17, which says:

12 Because I delivered the poor that cried, and the fatherless, and him that had none to help him.

13 The blessing of him that was ready to perish came upon me: and I caused the widow's heart to sing for joy.

14 I put on righteousness, and it clothed me: my judgment was as a robe and a diadem.

15 I was eyes to the blind, and feet was I to the lame.

16 I was a father to the poor: and the cause which I knew not I searched out.

17 And I break the jaws of the wicked, and plucked the spoil out of his teeth.

Reflecting on the tragedy of losing my sister Katlyn, I am still struck by how my mind shielded me during those difficult years, wrapping my emotions in a protective haze. That shield kept me safe then, and it continues to protect me today, though now in new ways and with a deeper understanding. Over time, I have come to see the profound influence of my coaches, not only on me but on countless others. Their steadfast values and unwavering love were blessings in disguise, shaping my life in ways I could never have foreseen.

Coaches stand at the crossroads of good and evil, playing a vital role in the healing of those they reach every day. My own healing began when my coaches took me under their wing in ninth grade. They helped me face wounds I thought were beyond repair, mending parts of me I did not even know were still raw. The identity they nurtured in me, the growth they cultivated, extend far beyond my years as a player. Even now, nearly two decades later, their lessons continue to echo in my heart, grounding me as both a man and a Christian.

At the beginning of this book, I wrote, *"I am thankful for our brain's remarkable ability to protect us during stressful times. It is astonishing how our minds help us adapt and shield us from emotions we cannot process, serving as a cherished defense mechanism."* Today, I understand something even greater: that God was with me all along, guiding me through those unimaginable moments, even when I did not recognize

His presence. He was there in every heartbreak, in every trial, faithfully carrying me when I could not carry myself.

God was with me that day in the cafeteria when my grandmother burst through the doors, weeping and crying my name. He stood beside me behind the school as I leaned against an electric pole, watching the CareFlight helicopter disappear into the sky. He was there as I painted that picture of a sailboat, unaware of the true magnitude of what was unfolding around me. Through every moment, He was present. His faithfulness sustained me, even when I could not see it. Truly, God is good.

To every coach reading this: keep fighting the good fight. Your work transforms lives in ways you may never fully grasp. And I promise you this, on Armageddon Day, it will all be worth it.

COACH'S REFLECTION

Reflecting on the excerpt above, consider how your role as a coach parallels the acts of service and justice described. Take some time to ponder the following questions:

- How do you embody righteousness and justice in your coaching practices, and how does this impact the individuals you serve?

- Are you actively seeking to "become eyes to the blind and feet to the lame" by addressing the specific needs of those who rely on your guidance?

- How do you approach advocating for and supporting those who may not have the strength or voice to stand on their own?

- What lessons can you take from this chapter about fighting against injustice or unfairness within your sphere of influence as a coach?

- Are you prepared to shatter the "fangs of the wicked" and protect those who are vulnerable, even when the path is difficult?

Take a moment to reflect on these questions and consider how your actions today can serve as a positive legacy for the future.

CHAPTER 13

HIDDEN IN THE MEMORIES

April 23, 2024, is quite a remarkable day I'll never forget. It marks the day I got baptized. It is a date that holds deep significance, as it came exactly 114 years after Theodore Roosevelt delivered his iconic *"Man in the Arena"* speech, and in many ways, I felt like I was finally stepping into my own arena. I am not sure why it took me so long to take that step, but after years of friends and family pouring into me in their own faithful ways, I knew the time had come.

For the first time, I truly understood the depth of grace and faith, particularly grace. I have learned how to extend grace, how to embrace it, and how to accept it in my own life. I am far from perfect, but I can say with certainty that this newfound understanding has transformed me for the better.

This book is not solely about football; it is about faith. It revisits the coaches who invested in me and focuses on the players we are all called to invest in today. It celebrates the joy that youth sports should bring, the honor inherent in the coaching profession, and the urgent need to evolve how we teach the game to align with how children learn.

It also addresses the critical role coaches play as guardians, especially in an era marked by broken systems, fractured homes, and fatherlessness. In many ways, coaches serve as the last line of defense for young men seeking direction, discipline, and love. This book stands against the darkness creeping into education, against the neglect of children who need strong role models, and for the restoration of mentorship through coaching.

We must take seriously the development of coaches, not only as instructors of the game but also as men of character. Coaches hold the keys to shaping futures. We honor them best not merely by remembering their lessons but by becoming the kind of coaches the next generation needs. This book is for those who coach with purpose, lead with love, and understand that football is just the beginning.

Upon reflection, I see how a common thread runs through much of my journey: football. The game has always been more than a sport to me. It has been a platform for building relationships, learning life lessons, and growing in faith. The coaches who shaped me were not just great at X's and O's; they were men of God who invested in their players' lives.

Coach Sam Harrell was not my position coach at Ennis, but his impact, along with the influence of the coaches he surrounded himself with, was undeniable. When I try to put into words what he meant to us players, how he carried himself, and how that translated into the broader coaching culture at Ennis, I honestly come up short. It is hard to capture the kind of presence of all of these coaches I love so much with just words.

That's been one of the more difficult parts about writing this book, trying to articulate not just facts or memories, but *meaning*. Finding the language that makes it all flow, that feels as true as it was when I lived it.

Recently, I was reminded of how mysteriously memory works. My family and I had just moved, and during the process, I came across some old scrapbooks. These were not just scrapbooks; they were pieces of my past, crafted by the people who loved me most. My sister had made some. My wife, who was my high school sweetheart back then, had made others. They were filled with newspaper clippings, photos, and notes from my playing days.

I am deeply grateful for those scrapbooks. They are more than paper and ink; they are time machines. That same day, I showed them to my kids, flipping through memories and laughing at the haircuts and oversized shoulder pads. And then something unexpected happened.

One of the old clippings had come loose, likely from years of storage in the garage or attic. I started to tuck it back in, intending to fix it later. But something made me pause. I turned the clipping over.

On the back was an article I had never noticed before. It was written by Sarah Stephens, the managing editor of the *Ennis Daily News* back in 2001. I didn't know her then. I was just a 17-year-old kid, worried about blocking the right guy, balancing schoolwork, and preparing for the next opponent. But her words from 24 years ago stopped me cold.

Her story was not a game recap or a breakdown of stats. It was something more reflective. More real. She wrote about arriving in Ennis as an outsider, not knowing who Coach Harrell was, and how, over time, her assumptions gave way to understanding. She saw him not just as a coach, but as a leader, a prayer warrior, and a steady, humble presence in the community.

When I read her words, it felt as if they had been waiting for me, hidden for 24 years. The article was about Coach Harrell, yet her description captured the spirit of every man who ever coached me at Ennis, men I love and respect deeply. Discovered by accident, tucked away among scrapbook memories, her piece expressed what I never could have put into words myself.

And that's the beautiful part. Though you are reading my book, at this moment you are hearing it through someone else's voice. Someone who did not grow up under the Friday night lights of Ennis. Someone who never stood in our locker room or weight room. Someone who lived in Ennis for only two years, yet still saw the truth clearly.

Sarah Stephens is a journalist. A real journalist. And that matters, because real journalism seeks to tell the truth without distortion or spin. After reading her article, I was struck by her work and wanted to know more. I searched online, hoping to reach out, and instead discovered a podcast she had joined.

Curious to hear her voice and get a sense of the person behind the words, I listened. In the podcast, Sarah shared her views on journalism, and her perspective deeply resonated with me. She said the **purpose of journalism is to give people the tools they need to be free**—free to think, to question, to decide for themselves. And she insisted that journalism should be **opinion-free and unbiased**, rooted in truth, not driven by agenda.

That's exactly what her article did. It didn't try to convince anyone of anything. It simply painted a picture. A moment. A man. In her article titled *"The Man with the Plan"* from the *Ennis Daily News* (2001), Sarah paints a deeply respectful portrait of Coach Sam Harrell. She begins by stating:

"Somehow, I thought he'd be bigger."

Sarah admitted she couldn't write a typical sports article and knew little about football. But that did not stop her from recognizing what truly mattered: Coach Harrell's character and impact. After hearing locals speak of him with admiration, she formed an image in her mind:

"I have to admit that picture included a large, loud man wearing a ballcap and coaching shorts, emphasizing sentences with a cuss word or two."

That stereotype did not last long. Her first real encounter with Coach Harrell came at Youthfest. Not on a sideline, but on a stage. And he was not giving a fiery pep talk. He was leading a prayer.

"For some reason I found myself surprised that the head football coach had been involved in such an event, and even more staggered by the fact he was up on stage leading a prayer."

Sarah contrasted her expectation of a tough, loud coach with the reality before her: a humble, faith-filled man whose quiet strength spoke louder than any whistle or playbook. What struck her most was how unusual it felt to see a coach pray with such sincerity.

"To envision them up on a stage praying with great emotion is not something that would spring to mind in any of my previous experiences."

What struck her most, and what she captured with remarkable clarity, was that Harrell's leadership extended far beyond football. He was, in her words, an "excellent man in the community," and she was "impressed."

Sarah Stephens's writing did not glorify Harrell with cliché or hype. Instead, she honored him by telling the truth, capturing a rare kind of leadership marked by humility, faith, and deep personal impact. The observations I stumbled upon years later, hidden on the back of a scrapbook clipping, carried even greater weight because they came from a journalist committed to truth, opinion-free, unbiased, and clear.

My coaches were not just experts at winning games; they knew how to build relationships and love players for who they were. They dedicated their lives to helping young men reach heights they could never have reached alone, using football as a vehicle to teach lessons that last long after the final whistle. Their leadership and example are exactly what we need more of in today's world.

As coaches, we hold a sacred responsibility: the chance to influence young lives. To honor the coaches who shaped us, we must carry forward their legacy, not simply by chasing victories but by shaping character. When I think of the men who inspired me, I ask myself: Would they be proud of the way I coach today? Would I welcome them to stand beside me on the sideline, listening to how I speak to my players? Would they see Christ reflected in my leadership? These questions matter far more than any play call or game plan. They remind us that the ultimate clock we face is not the one on the scoreboard but the clock of life. And when it reaches zero, each of us will have to answer for how we used our time.

I am not perfect, and I still have plenty of work to do. I know I need to pray more with Sarah, lead more prayers at the dinner table, and spend more time reading the Bible. I need to curse less, worship louder, and spend more time in one-on-one conversations with God. Yet this is what grace is truly about: recognizing our imperfections and returning to God again and again, doing our best to stay close to His word. Being a Christian is not about being flawless; it is about fighting the good fight, even when we stumble and fall short.

To every coach reading this, be proud to be an "Armageddon Coach," someone who invests in young people the way others once invested in you. Protect and honor the profession by living and leading in a way that reflects the values of those who inspired you. The legacy we leave is not measured in wins and losses but in the lives we touch and the seeds we plant along the way. Keep fighting, keep leading, and keep shining God's light for the next generation.

That is the real victory.

AFTERWORD

THE 10 TRUTHS OF BEING AN ARMAGEDDON COACH

THE GAME IS BIGGER THAN WINS AND LOSSES

A good coach knows football is a tool, not the ultimate prize. The lessons of teamwork, accountability, and discipline shape players for life, long after the lights turn off on Friday nights. *Armageddon Coach* reminds us that the scoreboard fades, but the relationships and character built under your leadership echo for decades.

LOVE IS STRONGER THAN KNOWLEDGE

Players rarely remember the technical details of a scheme, but they never forget how a coach made them feel. Love, respect, and authentic care become the foundation of trust. Coaching is teaching, but it is also fathering, mentoring, and guiding young men to believe they matter. Knowledge without love is hollow, but love makes knowledge stick.

GRIT STILL MATTERS

In a culture where entitlement often threatens perseverance, a good coach must fight to preserve grit. Struggle, sacrifice, and hard work must remain non-negotiable. As you teach players to push past pain and stay loyal to the team, you prepare them not only for football battles but also for life's trials. Grit is the antidote to softness.

LEADERSHIP REQUIRES COURAGE

Coaching is not for the faint of heart. Leadership means making unpopular decisions, demanding standards that stretch players, and standing firm when culture pushes back. It means correcting rather than coddling and having the courage to challenge athletes to become more than they think possible. Authority without courage breeds weakness, but courage inspires transformation.

MODERN LEARNERS NEED MODERN TEACHING

Generation Z athletes are different; they learn through visuals, feedback loops, and bite-sized lessons. A good coach adapts without lowering standards. Tools like WARDBORD remind us that coaching today must meet players where they are: on-demand, digital, and interactive. Conserving the profession means learning how to teach modern learners while holding on to timeless truths.

FEEDBACK IS MORE VALUABLE THAN FILM ALONE

Watching film without dialogue and direction becomes a passive experience. A good coach delivers feedback that is immediate, clear, and actionable. Grading execution and effort, pointing out both strengths and weaknesses, and creating teachable moments transforms film into growth. Knowledge dumping overwhelms, but timely, digestible feedback develops football IQ and player ownership.

COACHES ARE GUARDIANS

A coach's role goes far beyond X's and O's. Coaches are guardians of the culture, the standard, and the hearts of their players. They protect against the erosion of values, shield players from destructive outside influences, and stand in the gap for fatherless kids. Coaching is guardianship, and it is sacred work that demands vigilance and heart.

FAMILY BALANCE IS ESSENTIAL

Too many coaches lose themselves in the grind, sacrificing family on the altar of football. *Armageddon Coach* challenges this status quo: balance is not weakness; it is wisdom. By protecting your own marriage and children, you multiply your impact. Players respect a coach who models wholeness, not burnout. Football is important, but family is eternal.

FAITH AND PURPOSE FUEL LONGEVITY

Coaching without purpose leads to burnout. A good coach grounds his work in faith, conviction, and the belief that God uses coaches to impact lives. Purpose steadies you when the profession feels thankless, when losses pile up, or when controversy strikes. Faith reminds us that coaching is not just a job; it is a calling.

COACHING IS CONSERVATION

Every coach is a steward of the game and the profession. The way you coach today shapes what the profession will look like tomorrow. Will it be defined by quick fixes, selfishness, and distraction, or by grit, love, and purpose? A good coach preserves the best of coaching, passing down timeless values so the next generation can experience the same life-changing impact.